MW01169114

10 THINGS EVERY JEW SHOULD KNOW

BEFORE THEY GO TO COLLEGE

Griffith Moon

10 THINGS EVERY JEW SHOULD KNOW

BEFORE THEY GO TO COLLEGE

EMILY SCHRADER   **BLAKE FLAYTON**

EDITED & ILLUSTRATED BY

KIMBERLY BROOKS

10 Things Every Jew Should Know Before They Go To College
An Illustrated Guide
By Emily Schrader and Blake Flayton
Edited and Illustrated by Kimberly Brooks
Copyright © 2025 All rights reserved.

Hardcover Ingram ISBN: 978-1-7367738-5-7 Amazon ISBN: 978-1-7367738-6-4
Paperback Ingram ISBN: 978-1-7367738-9-5 Amazon ISBN: 978-1-7367738-7-1
eBook ISBN: 978-1-7367738-8-8

Library of Congress Control Number: 2025931489
10ThingsEveryJewShouldKnow.com/bibliography

Cover Design by Heather Sue Tokarsky
Book Layout and Typesetting by Heather Sue Tokarsky
Printed in the United States of America
First Printing, 2025

Published by Griffith Moon
Los Angeles, California
www.GriffithMoon.com

For large orders:
10thingsEveryJewShouldKnow.com/bookorders

For resources, events, and inquiries:
10ThingsEveryJewShouldKnow.com

DEDICATION

This book is dedicated to the 251 hostages taken by Hamas from their communities and homes on October 7th, 2023, to the hostages who have died in Hamas captivity since then, and to those who are still in Gaza waiting to be rescued.

ACKNOWLEDGEMENTS

This book would not have been possible without the wisdom, support, and dedication of several remarkable individuals.

First and foremost, as editor, I would like to acknowledge the immense contributions of authors Emily Schrader and Blake Flayton, both extraordinary thinkers at the vanguard of fighting for the truth about Israel and the Jewish people. I had admired their work for years when I approached them to collaborate on this project. Having two children in college at the time of this book's inception, I was growing increasingly concerned about what they and all college students were experiencing and learning when they arrived. I was struck by Blake's urgent warning, published in *The New York Times* in 2019, about the hostile environment he faced as a progressive Jewish student. His writings and commentary have since become an essential resource for understanding the challenges Jewish students encounter.

I was equally impacted hearing the story of Emily's experience as a history major at a major university, where —within mere weeks of arriving on campus—she was confronted by a towering "apartheid wall," an art installation designed to indoctrinate students with falsehoods about Jews and Israel. This experience ignited a fire in her to become a journalist and a fierce advocate, not just for Jews, but also for the oppressed people of Iran, who suffer under the same kind of authoritarianism that Israel's and America's enemies seek to impose. Like so many others, I remain deeply grateful for both Emily and Blake, whose relentless efforts to debunk falsehoods and present cold, hard facts—across television, print, and social media, in multiple languages—continue to illuminate truth on the global stage.

We extend our deepest gratitude to three exceptional experts whose scholarship profoundly influenced this book: Einat Wilf, whose groundbreaking work, *The War of Return*, provided a crucial and much-needed perspective on the Israeli-Palestinian conflict. Gil Troy, whose writings—including the new edition of *The Zionist Ideas*—have helped shape and inspire both the ancient and modern Zionist movement. And Zohar Raviv, Education Director at Birthright, whose unparalleled wisdom in Jewish and Israeli history enriched our approach to presenting these complex topics. Their insights, scholarship, and guidance provided invaluable clarity, helping to shape the way we framed this book's essential information.

A special thank you to Raiona Gaydos, whose meticulous eye and commitment to precision elevated every page, ensuring a seamless reading experience. We are also deeply grateful to Sadie Hilf, whose tireless efforts in gathering, verifying, and sourcing key information were instrumental in bringing this project to life. And a heartfelt thank you to Heather Sue Tokarsky for her beautiful and thoughtful layout design.

Finally, we extend our deepest appreciation to the courageous members of the Israeli and Jewish communities who work relentlessly to shine a light on the truth in the face of relentless distortions. Their bravery, resilience, and unwavering commitment to preserving history and confronting misrepresentation serve as a beacon of inspiration. Their efforts—both seen and unseen—lie at the very heart of this book.

To all of you: **Thank you**. Your contributions not only made this book possible, but also give it purpose.

Kimberly Brooks

INTRODUCTION

Despite sensing a rise in antisemitism in general, Jews around the world were still blindsided by the reaction on college campuses and in streets of major cities to the October 7th Massacre of 2023. College students are confronted daily with discrimination and false information, bombarded with demonizing rhetoric and skewed facts often reframed within identity politics wherein the Jewish people are labeled as oppressors. Conspiracy theories fomented within Middle East Studies departments underwritten by foreign governments only make matters worse.

This assault is all the more effective given that too many diaspora Jews know very little about being Jewish, their history spanning millennia, or even where their cultural values come from. Young Jews, now more than ever, need basic literacy in geopolitics, Middle Eastern history, and media bias to even begin to argue let alone combat the lies they may encounter on and off the campus.

The latest phenomenon of antisemitism on American college campuses has been brewing steadily over decades even though it seemed to burst immediately after October 7th, 2023. Many people who attended college in the 1970s and 1980s might find it hard to believe, as they may not have experienced one such incident in their entire lives. But starting in the 1990s, college students began to hear a distant anti-Zionist drumbeat grow ever louder, infiltrating subjects even outside history and politics. Often led by a faculty armed with revised text books, key elements of the Jewish Identity—Israel and Zionism—are pitted against the supposed values of polite, progressive society. Jewish culture has been recast as racist, and Jewish self-determination as colonialist.

This book provides a brief overview of Jewish culture and the subjects pertaining to the Middle East so commonly brought up on the quad today. It is by no means a complete history of the Jews or the Middle East, but offers a reference manual and guide to help Jewish college students reality-check and stand their ground when facing thorny subjects. The extensive bibliography can be found at 10ThingsEveryJewShouldKnow. com/bibliography. In addition to arming students with the information they need to counter antisemitic lies, 10 Things Every Jew Should Know also seeks to encourage students to reassert their Jewish values, ideas, and ideals that have constituted Jewish life and culture for millennia. While this book is written with a Jewish student audience in mind, it is suitable for people of all ages and faiths so that they too can be better informed.

For a complete bibliography, resources, events, and more, visit: **10ThingsEveryJewShouldKnow.com**

HOW THIS BOOK IS ORGANIZED:

1 **Who Are You**
A brief history of the Jewish people, different types of Jews, and an overview of what it means to be Jewish.

2 **Israel: The Nation**
A brief overview of Israel today, the land, the people, the history, and the movement for Jewish independence: Zionism.

3 **The Neighborhood (The Middle East)**
A brief historical and geopolitical survey of Israel's neighbors in the Middle East.

4 **The Big O (The Occupation)**
A review of the origins of "the occupation," the players, and how it manifests itself today.

5 **The Stick Up**
An examination of how foreign money, in the name of helping "refugees," funds terrorism in the region.

1

WHO ARE YOU?

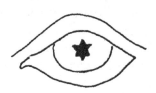

What does it mean to be a Jew?

The word Jew sounds similar in almost every language: "Judio" in Spanish, "Juden" and "Juif" in German and French (respectively), "Yahood" in Arabic, and "Yo" in Chinese.

The word Jew comes from Judah, later **Judea**, the name of the ancient kingdom that predates the modern **State of Israel** by 3000 years.[1] In this land, beginning at around 1200 B.C.E., the native people developed a unique way of life with their own calendar, holidays, religion and language, and a shared sense of history and destiny. Contrary to myths, Jews today come in every color imaginable and nearly every existing ethnicity. The Jewish holy book, **the Torah**, which goes by many other names, became the introductory text for both Christianity and **Islam**, and serves as the reason for Jews to be commonly known as the "People of the Book."

To be Jewish is to descend from an ancient and storied civilization. It is to be part of a people, a tribe, a culture, a nation, an ethnicity, and a religion, all at once. The Jews are one of the oldest peoples in the world, surviving their oppressors:

the Greeks, the Romans, the Germans, the Soviets, and those among the Muslim armies and terrorist organizations that routinely attack Israel. The Jews have been both admired and reviled in the societies in which they have resided, often to their peril. But they have still managed to thrive and uphold their most venerated values.

Whether a Jewish person lives in Israel, America, Australia, or France; whether a Jewish person only eats *kosher* and prays every morning or simply knows that their family history connects them to the tribe, a Jew is no less Jewish based on their observance, and one does not cease being Jewish simply because they don't practice the religious aspects of the faith. The canvas of Jewish life stretches far beyond its religious expressions, offering a multitude of ways to identify and engage with Jewish life. In short: A Jew is a Jew is a Jew.

BASIC STATISTICS

Jews make up just **0.2%** of the world's population. Yes, you heard that right. If the world consisted of one thousand people, only two would be Jewish! The proportion of American Jews is larger but still a mere 2% of the population.[2] Despite this, respondents in American surveys believed that America was 30% Jewish (!) -- fifteen times the actual number. Similar surveys revealed that people in countries from all over the world believe that the world is at least 10% Jewish.[3] Why do people harbor this misconception? Because Jewish peoples' work ethic and culture often lead to their disproportionately high representation in science, the arts, commerce, academia, law, and media.[4] Currently, the two largest Jewish communities are in the state of Israel, with a population of about 7 million Jews, and the United States, with a population of about 6 million Jews. There are also sizable Jewish populations in France (~450,000), Canada (~350,000), the UK (~300,000), Argentina (~180,000) and Russia (~150,000).[5]

A BRIEF HISTORY OF THE JEWS

In the Beginning
The **Hebrew Bible** begins with the creation of the universe by one God. Judaism largely introduced to the world the concept of **monotheism**.

Abraham and Sarah Set Forth
The Jewish people trace their lineage back to Abraham and Sarah, a couple from Ancient Mesopotamia who were commanded by God to *Lech Lecha*, "go forth into the land which I have promised to you and all of your descendants."[6] This statement records the birth of **Zionism**, the inherent bond between Abraham, Sarah, and their descendents with the land which will eventually be named after their grandson "Israel" (Jacob), and informs the entire history of the Jewish people from that point on. Abraham and Sarah's son Isaac marries Rebekah, then Isaac and Rebekah's son Jacob marries Leah. These are the Matriarchs and Patriarchs, the first Jews to live in the Land of Israel (then called Canaan).

The Jews Become Strangers in Egypt
Joseph, son of Jacob, is sold into slavery by his brothers and taken to Egypt. Soon, Joseph becomes the second in command of the Pharaoh's court, and soon after, the entire family of Jacob settled along the Nile to escape the famine ravaging Canaan. Several generations later, Joseph's descendants become enslaved by the polytheistic Pharaohs. But despite their subordination, the Canaanites, soon to be called "Israelites," kept faith in one God.

Exodus, The Story of Passover

Jews tell the story of Passover during a feast every spring, wherein the Jewish prophet Moses asks Pharaoh to "Let my people go." Finally, after a series of ten terrible plagues, Pharaoh agrees to let the Jews go. The Book of Exodus documents the Israelites leaving slavery in Egypt, and Moses's parting of the Red Sea that opens passage into the Promised Land — another seminal chapter in the evolution of Zionism as a pivotal Jewish value. The Passover celebration therefore ends with the shout: "Next Year in Jerusalem!"

Becoming a Nation

The Israelites wander the desert for forty years. God gives Moses the **Ten Commandments** at Mount Sinai, and henceforth, the children of Israel become a nation of their own with a land of their own. Once the land is conquered some time after Moses's death, it is divided among twelve tribes, named after the children of Jacob: **Reuben, Simeon, Levy, Judah, Dan, Naphtali, Gad, Asher, Issachar, Zebulun, Ephraim, Manasseh, and Benjamin.**

Israel Builds the First Temple

Once in the land, the Israelites begin to build their own civilization, centered around the Torah, or "the five books of Moses," which tells the story of their forefathers, foremothers, and the miracles and belief in one God. They form their own language, Hebrew (**Ivrit**, meaning, "on the other side of the water"), customs, and calendar, and build the **First Temple** circa 965 B.C.E., where all worship to God takes place. It is here when one of the most iconic Jewish kings rules the land, **King David**, who makes **Jerusalem** his capital. There is intense civil conflict amongst the Jews in this era. The people fight each other over and over again, eventually splitting the land into two separate kingdoms: **Israel and Judah**.

A BRIEF HISTORY OF THE JEWS (CONT.)

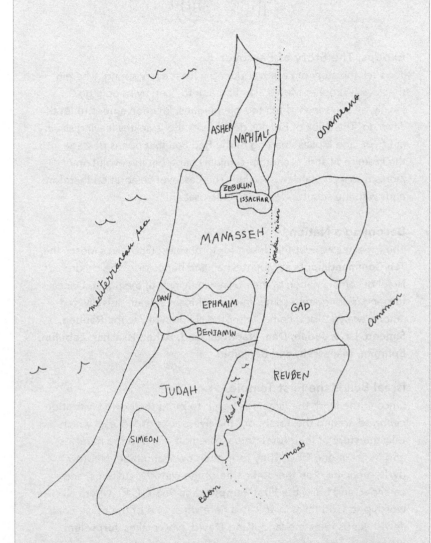

TERRITORIES OF THE TWELVE TRIBES OF ISRAEL C. 1200 B.C.E.

The First Temple is Destroyed

The **Babylonian Empire** invades the land and destroys the First Temple in 586 B.C.E.. This is remembered as one of the greatest tragedies in Jewish history, commemorated each year on **Tisha B'av**. This is also the beginning of the first Diaspora, when Jews scattered about the earth, mainly in Babylon itself.

The Jews Rebuild

In 538 B.C.E., during the reign of the Persian King, **Cyrus the Great**, the Jews return to Jerusalem and are permitted to build the **Second Temple** on the site of the original that had been destroyed.

The Destruction of the Second Temple

The Roman Empire conquers the entire Mediterranean including Judah, renaming the land "Judea." After one too many rebellions by the Judeans against the Romans, the Romans violently smash the Judean fighters, sack Jerusalem, burn the Second Temple to the ground, and expel a great number of Jews from the land (circa 70 C.E.). This expulsion of Jews marks the end of Jewish sovereignty in the Land of Israel and the beginning of the existence of Jewish civilization in **The Diaspora**.

The Diaspora Continues

Banished from their homeland, the Jewish people show a remarkable talent for keeping their traditions and unique customs alive. Wise men called **rabbis**, who are learned in Torah, become the leaders of the scattered Jewish community, ruling on laws and creating social norms that last for generations. By continuing the way of life birthed in the land, the Jews never stopped believing that they would eventually be restored "to the land of their fathers and mothers."

A BRIEF HISTORY OF THE JEWS (CONT.)

The Rise of Antisemitism in Europe

Wherever Jews live, their ethics and culture bring commerce and community. When allowed, they intermingle with the surrounding society, and are quick to learn all kinds of languages and trade. Often, the Jews are relegated to a small area (**shtetl** in the countryside, **ghetto** in the city) where they largely keep to themselves. What we now know today as **antisemitism** (a word itself hateful toward Jews, as it was designed by German journalist Wilhelm Marr in the 1870s to mean dislike of a people "foreign" to Europe) usually becomes a problem when societies face moments of crisis, such as recessions, wars, famines, or plagues, and need someone to blame.[7] European antisemitism climaxed in **the Holocaust**, Germany's systematic murder of 6 million Jews from Europe, the Balkans, and North Africa between 1939 and 1945.[8]

Next Year in Jerusalem

In the late 1800s, the millennia-old belief that the Jews would one day be restored to Zion manifests in a political movement aptly called **Zionism**. The Zionist movement, building on 4,000 years of Jewish history and evolution, represents an effort to bring the Jews back to their ancient homeland and establish political independence in a modern context and as full members of the Family of Nations. Jews had been singing "Next Year in Jerusalem" for two thousand years, but this time, they make next year now, and begin migrating to **Eretz Yisrael** (the Land of Israel) in the hundreds of thousands. Also around this time, there is a huge migration of European Jews to the United States.

Rebirth of the Nation: Israel

In May of 1948, after centuries of expulsion and immigration, the Jewish people declare the independent state of Israel. Right after its birth, 99% of the Jews in the Middle East are expelled or flee from their home countries of Iraq, Syria, Lebanon, Morocco, Iran, Jordan, and Egypt– some of whose families had lived there for millennia, and migrate to the new Jewish state.[9]

TYPES OF JEWS OF THE DIASPORA

At every Jewish wedding, the couple concludes the service by smashing a glass, usually followed by a loud "**Mazel Tov!**" – Hebrew for "Good Luck!" or "Congratulations!" This is done to remind us of the destruction of the Second Temple in Jerusalem, two thousand years ago.[10] Jews may now look and sound quite different from one another, but this tradition emphasizes that we are united by shared ancestry, culture, traditions, and connection to the original homeland. A Jew with family from Poland and a Jew with family from Iraq will have more in common and feel more comfortable at a shared Shabbat service or Passover seder table than at a Polish or Iraqi cultural festival. Regardless of where they are in the Diaspora, Jews everywhere sing the same prayers on Friday night dinners and share the same stories and common values. Let's talk about the different types of Jews:

Mizrahi
Mizrahi literally means "Eastern" and refers to Jews whose families found themselves in the Middle East and parts of North Africa after the Babylonian/Roman conquest of Judea. The "Mizrahi" identity can encompass Persian, Yemenite, **Levantine** (the region which today encompasses Israel and the Palestinian territories), Moroccan, and Syrian Jewry, and includes unique customs and traditions born from both the ancient Land of Israel and from hundreds of years under Arab/ Muslim rule. Some Mizrahi Jewish families remained in the same Middle Eastern cities from the time of the First and Second Temples. After the establishment of the State of Israel in 1948, up to 850,000 Mizrahi Jews fled to Israel from various Middle Eastern countries.[11]

Sephardi

Sephardic Jewry comes from the Hebrew word "Safrad," meaning Spain. Sephardic Jews trace their ancestry to the countries of the Iberian Peninsula, Spain and Portugal, and also to countries that at one point or another were under Spanish/Portuguese rule, including many in South America like Brazil, Argentina, and Panama (not to say at all that the only Jews in these places are Sephardi....) Sephardi is also a common identity in parts of North Africa and the Middle East, considering many Jews in these parts trace their ancestry back to the expulsion of Spanish Jews in **1492**. Sephardic communities thrive all around the world today, in the Americas, Israel, and parts of Europe. The traditional Sephardic language, **Ladino**, is a combination of Hebrew and Spanish.[12]

Ashkenazi

Ashkenaz translates to "German" in Medieval Hebrew and refers to the population of Jews that settled in Western Europe after the Roman conquest of Judea. As the centuries progressed and antisemitism became deadly in France and Germany, Jews migrated eastward to what is now Russia and Ukraine. Most Ashkenazi Jews today have multiple ancestors who lived in **The Pale of Settlement**, a large swath of land within which Jews were allowed to live, which encompasses parts of modern day Russia, Poland, Ukraine, Lithuania, and Belarus. At the end of the nineteenth and beginning of the twentieth century, a massive wave of **pogroms,** violent riots and massacres against the Jewish people, devastated "The Pale," and millions of Jews were forced to flee, many to the United States. Today, Ashkenazim are the main Jewish ethnic group in America. The particular Ashkenazi language, **Yiddish**, a combination of German and Hebrew written in Hebrew characters, is mainly spoken today by devoutly religious Jews in pockets of New York and Israel. The vast majority of native Yiddish speakers were killed in the Holocaust.[13]

Beta Israel

Beta Israel or **Falashas** (wanderers) refer to Jews from Ethiopia who now overwhelmingly live in Israel. The Beta Israel trace their ancestry back to the migration of one of the original Jewish tribes, the Tribe of Dan, from the Land of Israel to Ethiopia in the biblical era. Another timeline suggests that **King Solomon's** son, Menelik, who became the king of Egypt and married Makeda, Queen of Sheba, began Jewish tradition in Ethiopia, but various conquests and wars rendered the Jewish community relatively small and isolated.[14] In the 1990s, a massive initiative dubbed **Operation Solomon** consisted of airlifting tens of thousands of Ethiopian Jews to Israel.[15]

Bukharian

Bukharian Jews descend from a Diaspora community that formed in Central Asia after the destruction of the Second Temple. Bukharian culture brings with it a unique and vibrant style of dress, food, and language, Judeo-Tajik, a combination of Hebrew and Tajik, a form of Persian. Bukharian Jews used to refer to themselves as "B'nai Israel," which specifically meant the Jews who were subverted under the Assyrian Empire in ancient times. After the dissolution of the **Soviet Union**, most Bukharian Jews emigrated to Israel.[16]

Kavkazi

Also known as "Mountain Jews," **Kafkazi** Jews descend from Persia and the surrounding lands, known to be the direct descendants of the ancient Persian Jewish community who lived under Babylonian captivity after the destruction of the First Temple. The specific Kafkazi language, Judeo-Tat, is an ancient southwestern Iranian tongue combined with many elements of Hebrew.[17]

Desi Jews

Desi Jews are one of the earliest religious minorities to have lived in India. Some say they arrived during the biblical era and others say even earlier. Their population was as high as 50,000 in the early 1900s, but most immigrated to Israel after its establishment. Today there are seven Jewish communities in India, the most known being the *Bene Israel*. The Cochin Jewish community, which was highly involved in international trade well into the modern era, is said to have arrived in India after the destruction of the Second Temple.[18]

Kefkeng

Yes, there are even Jews from China! Scholars debate when the presence of a small Jewish community arose in the far east. Some trace it back to the seventh century or even earlier. Thousands of Jews managed to keep their traditions and customs in China for hundreds of years, until the idea of a unified, communist China began to take shape, and the Jews began to assimilate into wider Chinese society. However, there are a few Chinese people today who are miraculously discovering their Jewish roots.[19]

Just Jewish

The State of Israel has created a home for the Jews of the Diaspora to return to, to **make** *aliyah*, meaning "to rise up." As such, Israel has become the ultimate melting pot of Jewish identity and heritage. Whether it was the Ashkenazi Jews fleeing Europe before and during The Holocaust or the hundreds of thousands that fled the pogroms of the Middle East, Israel offered safe haven to all. Today, fewer Jews in Israel fall into one ethnic category. They are simply known as "Israelis."

A REAL CONVERSATION I'VE HAD A MILLION TIMES

-Isaac De Castro @isaacdecastrog on X

What's your ethnicity?
I'm Jewish.
But you're also hispanic?
I'm Latino, Panamanian.
So, you're also part Israeli?
No, I'm not.
It's not the same?
No, Israeli is a nationality and Jewish is a religion and ethnicity.
So you're half Panamanian and half Jewish?
No, I'm not—
So you're fully Jewish on both sides?
I am.
Then how are you Panamanian?
You know how Jews came to America from Europe or the Middle East? Some of them went to other places, and my family ended up in Panama.
But how can you be Panamanian if you're ethnically Jewish?
You know how American Jews are also Americans? Like that.
Why is your English so good?
I'm going to exit this conversation now.

THE GREAT JEWISH BOOK CLUB

Every week, Jews from around the world read the same Torah portion known as a **parshah**, and depending on how religious one is, spend time dissecting and parsing every word and hidden meaning. This has been happening without cessation for thousands of years. When a Jewish child comes of age at twelve or thirteen at their **bar mitzvah** (male) or **bat mitzvah** (female), they will read from the Torah for the first time in front of a large audience of friends and family. If someone is Jewish and has not gotten a bar or bat mitzvah yet, fear not, they can do this at any age. Many go to Israel and conduct the service at the **Wailing (Western) Wall**, or *Kotel.*

THE HEBREW BIBLE

The greatest book ever written – part history, part spiritual roadmap, part legal instructions-- the Hebrew Bible is divided into three sections: the Torah, also known as **The Five Books of Moses**, the **Prophets**, *"Nevi'im,"* and **Writings**, *"Ketuvim."* The acronym for these three letters is the T-N-K, or **"Tanakh."** The Hebrew Bible was locked in word for word sometime around

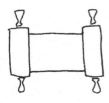

The Torah
The Torah describes the history of the Jews from the beginning of the world to Moses receiving the manuscript from God on Mount Sinai, and includes 613 commandments. The Torah ends with the death of Moses, when the Jews are still in the desert. There are five distinct sections: Genesis, Exodus, Leviticus, Numbers and Deuteronomy. The form read to this day most likely was adapted during 6th–5th century B.C.E., during the Babylonian Exile.

100 C.E. and has been replicated by trained scribes exactly the same way every time since. "Jerusalem" is mentioned 669 times in the Tanakh and **Zion** (another word for Jerusalem) is mentioned 154 times.[20] "Israel" is mentioned over two thousand times.

The Prophets, or "Nevi'im"

The Prophets cover the entrance of the Israelites into the Land of Israel until the Babylonian conquest in the 6th Century B.C.E.. There are two sections: the Former Prophets, which includes Joshua through 2 Kings, and the Latter Prophets, which contains the writings of three major prophets, Isaiah, Jeremiah, and Ezekiel, as well as twelve minor prophets. The stories explain history and foreshadow later events.

Writings, or "Ketuvim"

The final section of the Tanakh, "writings," includes the holy books of Ruth, Esther, Lamentations, and the Song of Songs. Jews ritually recite these different books at different times of year. For example, during Purim, the Book of Esther, or the **Megillah**, is read, which tells the story of a Jewish queen defeating a plan to kill all the Jews of Persia. On Tisha B'Av, Lamentations, or **Eicha**, is read, to commemorate the fall of the Holy Temples.

THE TALMUD

After the scripture of the Torah was completed and compiled into one never-changing version, Jewish scholars began to document the debates and discussions surrounding its stories and texts, the wisdom of which, until that point, had been passed down from generation to generation by word of mouth: the Oral Torah, also known as the **Mishnah**. The Torah and the Mishnah served as the platform upon which Jewish sages compiled the **Talmud**, a magnum opus, which for many centuries provided the central guidelines for Jewish life and overall education.[21] Two Talmuds were compiled during the 4th-6th centuries C.E.: the first was the **Jerusalemite Talmud**, composed by Jewish sages who managed to remain in the Land of Israel under foreign rulers and whose chief focus was the religious rulings pertaining to the Land of Israel itself; and the second (and far more voluminous) was the **Babylonian Talmud**, which touches on virtually every aspect of Jewish life. The Talmud created our modern understanding of **Rabbinic Judaism**, and today, millions of Jews all over the word study its teachings and use them to inform daily life. The majority of the Talmud was originally written in Aramaic, a now extinct language widely spoken in the Levant after the Roman conquest of Judea.

THE "ABRAHAMIC" RELIGIONS

Judaism
Even though Jews are a tiny minority, it is easy to take for granted the impact that the Torah has had on the global population. Indeed, Christianity and Islam both used the Hebrew Bible, which begins with Abraham's journey to the Promised Land, as inspiration for their particular books (the **New Testament** and the **Qu'ran**).

Christianity
In the third century B.C.E., the Hebrew Bible was translated into Greek and became an instant best-seller. The book was especially attractive to a young Jewish man named Jesus of Nazareth. A hundred years after Jesus' birth, Paul, one of his followers, wrote of his teachings in what would be called the New Testament, a (much smaller) sequel to the Hebrew Bible. The Christian Bible re-orders the Tanakh and adds a section on the life and works of Jesus Christ.

Islam
In the 600s, in the land of what is now known as Saudi Arabia, Mohammed emerged as a political, religious, and spiritual leader. The new faith of Islam was fashioned from the monotheistic teachings of Abraham, Moses, Jesus, and other prophets. Mohammed went to Medina, a city with a thriving Jewish community in Arabia, to recruit the Jews to the new religion. According to Muslims, Mohamed received prophecies from the prophet Gabriel that would eventually comprise the Qu'ran, or the Muslim Holy Book. This was also a best-seller in its time. In the Qu'ran, Jesus is mentioned 108 times, Moses is mentioned 136 times, Israel 43 times, and Jews are referred to as "the Children of Israel."[22]

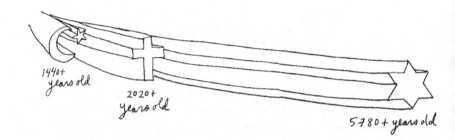

1440+ years old

2020+ years old

5780+ years old

THE JEWISH CALENDAR AND AGE OF RELIGIONS

The Jewish calendar is a lunar calendar dating back to the ancient Land of Israel. The beginning of the calendar is marked with **Rosh Hashana**, literally "head of the year." In the year 2024 as of this writing, the Jewish year is **5784**. When Christ was born, the Christians made that year zero (even though to Jews it was 3750). This also means that any time period before Christ was born goes backwards as if you're at the center of an algebraic numerical scale. The Islamic Calendar is also lunar and starts at the birth of Mohammed, making the Islamic year for 2024, 1445.

The State of Israel still uses the Jewish calendar to arrange its important days, even days that are not included in the Torah, such as **Yom Ha'atzmaut**, the Israeli Day of Independence, and **Yom HaShoah**, Holocaust Remembrance Day, which in the Hebrew calendar marks the anniversary of the **Warsaw Ghetto Uprising**.

JEWISH VALUES

Jewish values keep the Jewish people together and are passed down from generation to generation. While they adapt with each new age, the bedrock remains the same. The Jewish people value life, justice, education, and service to humanity. They value family, food, music, tradition, and community. Then there are some differing values depending on which Jew you ask. An Orthodox Jew would tell you that Jewish values center around the 613 **mitzvot**, or commandments from God, which include praying in synagogue, fasting on Yom Kippur, and having children. Other Jews will emphasize the principle of **Tikkun Olam**, "healing the world," through social justice activism. Zionism is an integral value to Jews in Israel and in the Diaspora, with some even choosing to *make aliyah* (moving to Israel.) Regardless of one's background, level of observance, or different perspectives, the Jewish people bear responsibility for each other. Perhaps that is the highest value of them all.

THE TEN COMMANDMENTS

The Ten Commandments comprise the foundational principles in the Jewish religion. The first four are about one's relationship with God and the last six are about one's relationship with people.

1. Thou shalt have no other gods before Me.

2. Thou shalt not make gods or worship them (Idolatry).

3. Thou shalt not use the Lord's name in vain.

4. Thou shalt keep the Sabbath Day holy.

5. Thou shalt honor thy father and mother.

6. Thou shalt not murder.

7. Thou shalt not commit adultery.

8. Thou shalt not steal.

9. Thou shalt not give false witness against thy neighbor.

10. Thou shalt not covet.

Monotheism

Once upon a time, most societies believed that each aspect of life had a different god, and praying to that particular god influenced life on earth. Judaism was a revolution in human affairs in that it entrusted all authority in one singular divine entity whose morals and values were all-knowing and all-encompassing.[23] This wrested the ultimate power away from the fickle gods of natural elements and animals. Christianity, and centuries later, Islam, both would not exist today had Judaism not given to the world the idea of one singular God. Today, thanks to the Jews, the majority of the world's population, 55% of people, follow a monotheistic religion.[24]

Justice, Compassion, Morality

Jewish tradition sees morality as something that's discovered through **dialogue with authority**, rather than mindless submission.[25] Thus, when God tells Abraham about his plans to punish the sinful cities of Sodom and Gomorrah, Abraham implores God to put the accused cities through a proper trial to determine whether any innocent people still dwell within them (it turns out there was only one).[26] In this act, Abraham represented the moral core of what will become Jewish justice: a willingness to question authority, a commitment to fairness and justice, a centering of human empathy and compassion, and the seeds of what we know today as due process. These principles are codified in Jewish law, form the basis of democracies, and even serve as a primary inspiration to the language of the Constitution of the United States.

Argumentation: Wrestling with God

"Two Jews, three opinions."

Jews are notorious for arguing and disagreeing. In Hebrew school, Jewish children learn about Jacob, one of the iconic Jewish forefathers, who wrestled with a man on the banks of a river in Canaan. After the fight, Jacob gives his name, but the man refuses to give his. He does, however, bless Jacob, calling him "Israel," saying: "Your name shall no more be called Jacob, but Israel, for you have striven (argued) with God and with men, and have prevailed."[27] Therefore, many directly translate "Israel" to mean "wrestling with God," a profoundly symbolic description of the nature of the Jewish people throughout history, and the complexities of the modern State of Israel today. To wit, the Talmud is a series of interpretations, a.k.a. "arguments," on how the law is applied.

No False Idols

From the earliest sparks of history, humans have been representing their experiences and memories with images. Depicting the great forces of the universe as idols and totems has been central to the development of civilization; deities were pictured walking the earth, taking the shape of men, beasts, or fantastical creatures. But Judaism would have none of that. "Thou shalt not make yourself an idol," commanded God. This wasn't just to ward off the worship of other gods, but a warning against creating a physical representation of the infinite.

To Be Human is Divine

The word, "human," comes from the Latin, "humus," meaning ground or earth.[28] Adam comes from "adama," also meaning earth.[29] The first chapter of the Torah proclaims that Adam is made in the image of God (and if you read carefully, you find that both the man and the woman were created in God's image — Genesis 1-27) — you know, that infinite, perfect being that makes and powers the cosmos — and moral history was never the same again. Liberalism, humanism, individualism, socialism... all the isms of Western thought stemmed from this single idea: Humanity is divine. Before Judaism, people conducted child and virgin sacrifice to show ultimate devotion to different gods. In the story of "The Binding of Isaac," when Abraham takes his oldest son to a mountaintop with the intent on sacrificing him, an angel stops him in his tracks: a completely revolutionary act in the history of humanity.[30] It was another way to say, "everyone is created in the image of God," a.k.a., "don't kill your kids."[31]

Love of Strangers

The story of Exodus, when the Jews were led from Egypt where they had been enslaved into the Land of Israel, forms the bedrock narrative of Jewish identity. Exodus also created the imperative to love the foreigner in your midst. "Remember that you were a stranger in a strange land," the Torah reminds the Hebrews.[32]

The Chosen People

What God meant by "choosing" his people has been the focus of debate for centuries. Some have explained it as a mission for the Jewish people, a duty to stand as a model for the other nations of the world.[33] Others say being chosen means nothing more than the burden of following the rules of the Torah. Still others think that "chosenness" means that God speaks to the world through the Jewish people – that is, the events that have happened to the Jews throughout history carry a universal message. Regardless of interpretation, it's important to note: chosenness does not mean superiority to any other group of people.

Holidays: "They Tried to Kill Us. We Survived. Let's Eat!"

Most Jews, regardless of how religious, know about the major holidays of Passover, which commemorates when the Jewish people fled Egypt, Hanukkah, the celebration of the Jewish revolt against the Greeks and the rededication of the Temple, and **Purim**, when the valiant **Queen Esther** revealed herself to be a Jew to the king of Persia and thus thwarted an attempt to massacre her people. Of course there are other holidays, such as **Sukkot**, **Simchat Torah**, and **Tu B'av**, the Jewish Valentine's Day, but the main take away from an overwhelming number of our stories is: don't mess with the Jews, we will outlive you.

THE STORY OF HANUKKAH

Hanukkah is often thought of in the United States as "the Jewish Christmas" because it usually falls around the time of Christmas, but the truth is this holiday isn't about presents or world peace, but about Jewish pride and a refusal to give in to occupiers who sought to eradicate the Jewish people. Hanukkah commemorates the rededication of the Second Temple in Jerusalem at the start of the revolt of the **Maccabees** against the Macedonian Greeks. The Maccabees were a group of rebels who resisted the religious coercion forced upon them by their imperial rulers, and fought for self-determination. In many regards, they are a model until today of early Zionism. The holiday is marked by lighting the menorah for 8 nights, each night adding an additional flame, to symbolize how the oil miraculously burned for 8 nights at the time the Jewish Temple was recovered.

Entertainment and Laughter

A byproduct of the constant ignition of their imaginations through storytelling, Jews have been known for their wit, humor, and intellect. Some believe that the Jewish ability to retort with a witty comeback after centuries of discrimination led to such a knack for entertainment and making people laugh. In part as a response to being excluded from certain industries as a result of antisemitism, Jews became foundational in the building of European and American showbusiness, such as cabaret, Vaudeville, Broadway, and then of course, Hollywood, which was a uniquely and wildly successful Jewish American enterprise. Jews were also instrumental in the creation of Bollywood in India.[34] Jews became a centerpiece of American comedy in the twentieth century, too, with one joke stating that in 1975, 80% of stand-up comedians were Jewish.

Connection to the Land

Because the Land of Israel has remained central to the Jewish people for thousands of years, and the only land in the entire world to be intrinsically associated with the Jewish people (which is the correct context of the term "Zionism"), so too does the Jewish state serve as an important marker of identity for the vast majority (around 90%) of Jews.[35] Those who are not living in Israel still find a way to incorporate the Jewish state into their lives by way of Zionism, the non-mutually exclusive belief that Jewish people have a right to a state of their own in their ancient homeland.

RELIGIOSITY

The Jewish people have an interesting relationship with the concept of religion. Jews always understood themselves to be a people, a nation, but in modern Europe, the **Enlightenment** gave birth to the notion that different peoples could be citizens of a multicultural country, and that Judaism could exist as a type of faith, separate from the nation.[36] Judaism was confined to an individual's spiritual beliefs rather than a community's unique customs and characteristics. The redefining of Judaism in this manner, classified by levels of religiosity, is more prevalent in the Ashkenazi Jewish community than in the others.

Orthodox
Orthodox Judaism refers to many different streams and sects within Judaism which include all those who value a strict understanding of Jewish religious law, ritual, and tradition. These rituals include wearing a small head covering called a **kippah** (also known as a **yarmulke**) if you're a man and a longer

Religiosity *(cont.)*
head covering if you are a married woman, keeping a kosher diet, studying Torah, raising children with a strong sense of religious identity, **wrapping tefillin** (black leather straps placed around the arm and head that are said to tether man to God) every morning, and placing prayer and a relationship with God above most all else. Orthodox Judaism is very popular in both North America and Israel, with rapidly growing communities in both countries. Examples of Orthodoxy include "**Modern Orthodox**," a blend of Orthodoxy and secular lifestyles (as featured in the Israeli show *"Srugim"*), and **Chabad**, a very popular stream of Judaism that follows the teaching of Rabbi Menachem Mendel Schneerson (see next page).

Reform
Reform Judaism was birthed in Central Europe in the 19th century as a Jewish response to the Enlightenment, the central doctrines of which were defined by individual liberty and religious tolerance. Early reformists sought to modernize Judaism by making its services in the native language instead of only Hebrew. Later, Reform Judaism introduced the concepts of female rabbis, the Bat Mitzvah, egalitarian prayer, LGBT incorporation, and *Tikkun Olam*: "healing the world" through social justice. Reform Judaism has been most popular in the United States, where it is widely seen as a complement to American culture, emphasizing individual liberty, progress, and incorporation of universal values
with faith.[37]

Reconstructionist
Founded by Rabbi Mordechai Kaplan, reconstructionism is a subset of the Reform movement. Reconstructionist Judaism is a generally new stream of Judaism in North America that views Judaism as an "evolving civilization."[38] Like reformism, reconstructionism centers on social justice and strives to adapt Jewish text into a metaphorical outlook on morality, progress, and humanity's role in an ever-changing world.

Conservative

Conservative Judaism is also a modern Jewish reaction to the Enlightenment, but it doesn't go as far as reformism. Conservative Jews value the blending of modernity with the traditional basis of Judaism, and again, it is a movement most common in North America. Like reformism, there are many who are working to establish a more prominent conservative movement in Israel and around the world.[39]

Hasidic and Haredi

Hasidic Judaism is a sect of Haredi Judaism, which is itself a sect of Orthodox Judaism. "Haredi" translates to one *who trembles*, referring to the act of shaking from devotion to God during prayer, and is the more general term for "Ultra-Orthodox" in Israel. *Hasidism* comes from a Jewish spiritual revival in Ukraine in the 18th century, a reaction to Jews who were becoming more secular and reformist.[40] Despite dressing in what looks to some like clothing from a bygone era, Hasids were considered the wild hippies of their time, wanting to reclaim the mysticism inherent within Judaism. Haredi Jews are prominently featured in the Israeli show *Shtisel*. Many Hasidic/ Haredi Jews today still speak Yiddish (a German dialect with words from Hebrew, Aramaic, and several modern languages), all value the *most strict* accordance to Jewish law and Torah, and most seclude themselves in culturally rich neighborhoods such as Brooklyn and Jerusalem. There are different sects of Hasidic Jews including the **Satmar** community, a Hungarian sect (as represented in the Netflix show "Unorthodox"), the Yeshivish, the Litvish, and more. Usually the divisions within the Hasidic community originate from the country of origin and the details of prayers and dress.

Atheist/Secular Jews

Some Jews do not believe in God or question the existence of God while following almost none of the principles laid out in the Torah, yet remain proud members of the Jewish community. Secular Jews have contributed a great deal to the Jewish story, such as legendary authors Franz Kafka, Ayn Rand, and Philip Roth, philosophers like Hannah Arendt and Karl Popper, scientists like Frank Oppenheimer and Albert Einstein, sociologists like Sigmund Freud, and legendary political leaders like Theodor Herzl, David Ben-Gurion, and Golda Meir. Many Jews who are not religious feel connected to their Jewish identity through family, community, and history, or by way of the state of Israel. In fact, in Israel, approximately 45% of the population is secular.[41] Jewish secularism is said to have begun with Baruch Spinoza, a Sephardic Jew in seventeenth century Amsterdam who proposed the idea of God as being synonymous with nature.[42]

CHABAD

Where you live, there is likely a local Chabad congregation that will always welcome you to a Shabbat dinner. Chabad is a division of Hasidic Judaism founded by **Rabbi Menachem Mendel Schneerson**, also known as the "Lubavitcher Rebbe." A unique project of the Rebbe was creating a Jewish outreach program to help Jews become more connected to their own religion. Chabad emissaries are typically seen on busy city streets, encouraging Jewish men to wrap tefillin and giving candles to women to light for Shabbat. This is not a mission of converting non-Jews, as proselytizing is against the Jewish religion. Instead, Chabad seeks to reconnect Jews with their Jewishness and with each other, wherever they are.

ALBERT EINSTEIN

I believe in Spinoza's God who reveals himself in the orderly harmony of what exists, not in a God who concerns himself with the fates and actions of human beings.

- Albert Einstein

Converts, A Small, Respected Minority

In addition to Jewishness showing up on a DNA test, Jews also *become* Jewish through conversion. In the biblical story of Ruth as the first Jewish convert, Ruth is revered for her devotion to God, and also the great grandmother of King David, making her the progenitor of Jewish monarchical lineage in the Torah. The process of converting to Judaism is not easy. Rabbis often turn a candidate away at least three times to test their conviction. Prospective converts begin by intensely studying Judaism: the history, religious texts, values, and customs. This process can be years long. Then, a Jewish court, or the *beit din*, will decide whether or not the convert can fully become a Jew, usually along with a pledge of solidarity with the Jewish people. Finally, the convert heads to the *mikvah*, or ritual bath meant to purify the body (very sacred in Judaism), says a blessing, and emerges from the water as a Jew. Once this is complete, the convert chooses a Hebrew name and hosts a celebration. It's important to note again that the Jewish people do not proselytize, meaning they do not actively seek out or encourage others to join the tribe. If a person upon their own volition wishes to become Jewish, it is up to them to see it through.

JEWS AND AMERICA

There are about 6 million Jews in America. If one is an American Jew, they might be one of the luckiest Jews in the history of the Jewish people, considering the freedom and prosperity offered by *"Der Goldene Medina,"* or, "The Golden Land," in Yiddish. The earliest Jews to arrive in what would become America were Sephardim from Brazil, who docked in "New Amsterdam," now New York, in the 1600s after being expelled during the Spanish Inquisition.[43]

In 1790, **George Washington** and **Thomas Jefferson** met multiple Jewish groups in Rhode Island while soliciting support for their twelve proposed amendments to the constitution (the Bill of Rights). Washington was so moved from his experience at the synagogue that he penned a formal letter to the "Jews of Newport" stating:

> *May the children of the stock of Abraham who dwell in this land continue to merit and enjoy the good will of the other inhabitants — while every one shall sit in safety under his own vine and fig tree and there shall be none to make him afraid.*

In a letter dated 1808, America's second president **John Adams** wrote of the Jews:

> *They are the most glorious nation that ever inhabited this Earth. The Romans and their Empire were built but a bauble in comparison to the Jews. They have given religion to three quarters of the Globe and have influenced the affairs of Mankind more and*

more happily than any other nation ancient or modern.... I will insist the Hebrews have done more to civilize men than any other nation....[44]

The history of the Jewish people and their values are woven into the fabric of America. The Hebrew Bible strongly influenced the founding fathers when writing the Declaration of Independence and the Constitution. Thomas Jefferson and **Benjamin Franklin** originally planned for the seal of the United States to depict the Jews leaving slavery in Egypt. The only inscription on the Liberty Bell is from the Hebrew Bible, Leviticus: "Proclaim Liberty Throughout All the Land Unto All the Inhabitants thereof."

Between 1880 and 1924, over 3 million Jews migrated from Eastern Europe to America to escape antisemitism (there were over 250 anti-Jewish pogroms in the Pale of Settlement between 1881 and 1884 alone).[45] Many of these Jews settled in big cities like New York, living lower class lives in crowded, unsanitary apartment blocks called tenements. The Jews of the **tenements** worked so hard to build a better future for their children and grandchildren which makes them a perfect example of fulfilling "The American Dream." The quote inscribed on the base of the Statue of Liberty honors this wave of migrants, as it was written by **Emma Lazarus** (1849-1897), a Sephardic Jewish American author and a fierce Zionist.

Give me your tired, your poor
Your huddled masses yearning to breathe free
The wretched refuse of your teeming shore
Send these the homeless tempest-tost to me
I lift my lamp beside the golden door
- Emma Lazarus

Jews and America *(cont.)*

But the American **philosemitic** sentiment did not last forever. In the early twentieth century, America fell prey to the insidious disease of antisemitism that engulfed Europe. Nazis with swastika-bearing arm bands marched in New York in the late 1930s, and more than 900 Jewish souls escaping from Germany lost their lives in concentration camps when the M.S. St. Louis was turned away from American shores.[46] Even socially, Jews were prohibited from working in many industries in America and were treated as second class citizens by certain segments of American society. Jews were also prohibited from membership in many clubs and organizations and faced quotas at top universities.[47]

In the 1970s, when the Iranian monarchy fell (which we'll discuss in later chapters), a wave of Persian Jews came to America, mostly to Los Angeles. In the 1990s, when the Soviet Union fell, a sizable wave of Russian Jewish immigrants arrived in America, a whole century after the first wave of Russian Jewish newcomers.[48]

JEWS IN THE MIDDLE EAST

After twenty five hundred years of Jewish communities in the Middle East, 99.9% of these Jews have been expelled, often gruesomely via pogroms, and are now mostly only in Israel.[50] Over 850,000 left their property and homes in a wave of antisemitism in the 1940s, when Israel was on the cusp of independence. There were other violent episodes in Iraq, Syria, Lebanon, Morocco, Iran, and Egypt, which resulted in the ethnic cleansing of Jews from the Middle East and the purging of their wondrous contributions to its culture. None of these countries have admitted their role in oppressing their Jewish populations, nor have they made reparations (more on this in later chapters).

JEWISH POPULATIONS	1948	2018
Algeria	140,000	<50
Egypt	75,000	100
Iraq	135,000	<10
Lebanon	5,000	<100
Libya	38,000	0
Morocco	265,000	2,150
Syria	30,000	2,150
Tunisia	105,000	1,050
Yemen	63,000	<50
Afghanistan	5,000	0

*The website *Diarna* (diarna.org) is an online "geo-museum" which works to preserve the physical remnants of Jewish life in the Middle East. Together with oral testimonies of Jewish life under Arab rule, *Diarna* provides fascinating visuals and a multitude of research for those wishing to go back in time.

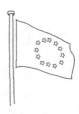

JEWS IN EUROPE

The Jewish story in Europe predominantly began after the destruction of the Second Temple and the expulsion of many Jews to the shores of the Roman Empire. For two-thousand years in Europe, Jews developed their own culture, secluded in small villages, called **shtetls** in the countryside and **ghettos** in major cities. This separation from larger society allowed for incredible spiritual enrichment and the sharpening of Jewish identity, but with it came antisemitism from Christians who believed the Jews collectively had killed Christ.[49] When modernity came and the walls of the ghetto tumbled down, many Jews became the model European citizens, contributing to every sector of life: business, the arts, science and medicine, national service, politics, and more. But European antisemitism merely evolved and Jews still faced a wave of persecution, culminating in the Holocaust, the systematic murder of 6 million Jews by the Nazi regime in Germany. Most Eastern European Jews who stayed perished in the Holocaust, but many made it to America, and some emigrated to the **Ottoman Empire** region of Palestine, now Israel. There are not nearly as many Jews in Europe today as before the Holocaust, but in the post-World War II age and with a Jewish sovereign state, Jewish life in Europe shines brightly, confidently, and rebelliously, most notably in places like Paris, Berlin, and Moscow.

A SMALL, ANCIENT, AND BRILLIANT MINORITY

Jews are part of an ancient, brilliant, and resilient civilization that was dispersed from a tiny piece of land thousands of years ago. About half the world's Jews have finally come back to the land in the last century. No matter where Jews are from or where they live, Jews who were born Jewish can trace their roots back to Israel. Even Ashkenazi Jews have more in common genetically with Sephardim and Mizrahim than they do with non-Jews from Poland or Russia.[52] Jews come in every color, and the size of the population is miniscule in relation to its impact on whichever society within which it resides. Antisemitism ebbs and flows: sometimes Jews are brought in to promote commerce and community, and other times they are cast out. However, despite what might be in the news or on social media feeds, today's Jews are in fact the luckiest and freest Jews ever to be alive since the time of the Second Temple.

2

ISRAEL

Israel, "the Jewish state," is the only country in the world in which the Jewish people comprise a majority.[53] Israel was *reborn* in 1948, at the same time as many other states around the world. As the Jewish state, Israel strives to reflect the values of the Jewish people. Israel balances being a safe haven for all Jews in the world and also being a liberal democracy where religious and ethnic minorities are protected by law. From Israel's **Declaration of Independence** in 1949:

> *The State of Israel...will ensure complete equality of social and political rights to all its inhabitants irrespective of religion, race or sex; it will guarantee freedom of religion, conscience, language, education and culture; it will safeguard the Holy Places of all religions....We appeal...to the Arab inhabitants of the State of Israel to preserve peace and participate in the upbuilding of the State on the basis of full and equal citizenship and due representation in all its provisional and permanent institutions.*[54]

In 1867, Jerusalem was a small city of 16,000 souls, which **Mark Twain** referred to as "mournful, and dreary, and lifeless."[55]

Tel Aviv was merely sand dunes. Arab Muslim villages were sprinkled throughout the deserts and seaside ports of the land, along with **Arab Christians, Greeks, Armenians, Kurds**, various Europeans, and of course, Jews. Jews were actually the majority population in Jerusalem in the 19th century, when those overseas began to take an interest in returning to the land.[56] Most within the city lived in crushing poverty and oppressive rule. In the 20th century, the land would undergo a transformation never before seen in modern history. What was old became new; what was seen as a dream became a reality.

DEMOGRAPHY

Israel has 9.3 million citizens, and as of 2023, the population is estimated to be around 73-74% Jewish. Every type of Jew there is can be found in Israel: Ashkenazim, Sephardim, Mizrahim, Beta Israel, Bukharian, and more, but as Israel is almost a hundred years old, many of these different types of Jews have blended together. The minority populations are divided between Muslims (82%), **Druze** (8%), and Christians (8%). The Druze follow an Abrahamic, monotheistic religion with unique spiritual beliefs, not unlike those of Jews. Christians are usually found in Jerusalem or in Israel's north. The Christian quarter in Jerusalem hosts many of their holiest sites, including the grand Church of the Holy Sepulchre, where Christ is believed to have been crucified (according to Orthodox Christianity). According to polls, most Arabs within Israel identify themselves as Israeli-Arabs and a much smaller minority, between 7% and 14% in recent polls, identify as **Palestinians**.[57]

MAJOR CITIES AND SITES

JERUSALEM

Jerusalem, also known as *Zion*, is the capital of Israel and has been "the capital of the Jewish people" for over three thousand years. In Jerusalem, King David, one of the earliest and most iconic kings of Judea, established his capital: the center of Jewish civilization. Both Jewish temples stood in Jerusalem, but today, all that is left of the Second Temple is the Western Wall. In Jerusalem, you will find holy sites for not just Jews, but for Muslims and Christians as well, both religious and artistic neighborhoods, lively markets, and the best food in Israel (according to many). Though Israeli leaders often say that Jerusalem is "united," the populations of West and East Jerusalem are split relatively evenly between Muslims and Jews, and tensions persist over the Old City, which lies in the center of West and East. Jerusalem, Zion, would become a major symbol for Jews around the world involved in the campaign to re-establish Jewish independence.

HATIKVA

As long as deep in the heart,
The soul of a Jew yearns,
And forward to the East
To Zion, an eye looks
Our hope will not be lost,
The hope of two thousand years,
To be a free nation in our land,
The land of Zion and Jerusalem.

- Stanza from *"Hatikva"* (*The Hope*), by Naftali Herz Imber, 1887, later to become Israel's national anthem.

THE DOME OF THE ROCK

THE WESTERN WALL

AL AQSA MOSQUE

The Temple Mount

At the heart of the Old City of Jerusalem is the **Temple Mount**, the holiest site in the world for Jews – where Abraham brought his son Isaac to sacrifice to God, but was held back by an angel, and where fragments of the First and Second Temple period are constantly uncovered: sometimes pieces of pottery, or coins imprinted with menorahs.[58] It is impossible to not feel the presence of history when peering over this famous spot.

The first Temple, built by King Solomon, stood for four hundred years before being destroyed by the Babylonians, a tragedy that Jews recall every year on *Tisha B'Av*. The Jews were held captive by the Babylonian empire until their eventual release and permission, at the hands of Persian King Cyrus the Great, to rebuild their Temple in 538 B.C.E.. A common psalm Jews recite to remember the Babylonian captivity:

> *By the rivers of Babylon, there we sat down, yea, we wept, when we remembered Zion. We hanged our harps upon the willows in the midst thereof. For there they that carried us away captive required of us a song; and they that wasted us required of us mirth, saying, Sing us one of the songs of Zion.*[59]

The Second Temple, known to be even grander than the first, also stood for about four hundred years, but was destroyed by the Romans after the Jews launched several failed rebellions.[60] Flavius Josephus, a Jewish scholar of the era who defected to the Roman ranks, described the Temple in his work *The Antiquities of the Jews*: "For the honor of God, with great variety and magnificence, sparing no cost... the temple which was beyond this [partition surrounding the Temple] was a wonderful one indeed, and such as exceeds all description in words; nay, if I may so say, is hardly believed upon sight..."[61] The Romans commemorated the sacking of Jerusalem in the famous Arch of Titus in Rome, where Roman soldiers are depicted carrying away Jewish treasures, including a menorah. For centuries, the Temple Mount stood empty, without any structure built atop it, intentionally kept that way as a monument to the defeat of Jewish civilization.

The Dome of the Rock and Al-Aqsa Mosque

The Dome of the Rock is the large golden dome featured in so many pictures of Jerusalem, built intentionally on the site of the Temple Mount during the Muslim conquests after the death of Mohammed in the 7th century. It was the common practice of Muslim conquerors to build their holy sites over the holy sites of others as a method of asserting dominance.[62] During the Crusades, circa 1099, the Knights of Templar used the Dome as a military headquarters, but it was recaptured by Muslim armies a hundred years later. The Dome of the Rock is not a mosque, but rather a shrine to mark where Muslims believe the Prophet Mohammed had a "night journey" - a dream where he met the prophets Abraham, Moses, and Jesus in heaven. The large platform on which the Dome sits is also home to the **Al-Aqsa Mosque**, a place of worship several meters to the south. People often confuse the Dome of the Rock with Al-Aqsa Mosque. The exact significance of the site of Mohammed's "night journey" has changed over the centuries, as neither Jerusalem nor the Temple Mount is mentioned in the Qur'an. Today, access to this sacred site is unrestricted to Muslims, while Jews must follow a set of behavioral and time limits, a source of great controversy in Israel.[63]

The Western Wall

"**The Western Wall**," "**The Wailing Wall**," or simply, "**The Kotel**", an ancient Hebrew word for *wall*, is recognizable to Jews around the world. This sacred place is the only remains of the retaining wall surrounding the Temple Mount, the site of the First and Second Temples of Jerusalem. Jews come here to connect to a greater power, celebrate holidays, pledge military service to the country, and sometimes, to simply dance – to find joy in the freedom of being a Jew today. But throughout history, the Wall was where Jews came to weep, to wail, to commemorate the horrible loss of both Temples. The comparison between the mood at the Kotel today versus before the establishment of Israel is two different worlds.

TEL AVIV

The best example of forward-thinking Israeli society is the city of **Tel Aviv**, known for its beaches, secular and bohemian culture, nightlife, theaters, sports, architecture, high-tech start-ups, food, skyscrapers, and religious diversity. Right in Tel Aviv's backyard is the Arab-majority city of Yafo, bustling with its own unique culture. At its founding in 1909, Tel Aviv was merely sand dunes – its first Jewish immigrants drew lots to decide who would be given which area of the land to build upon. This first neighborhood of legend is now known as Neve Tzedek, home today to a lively French-Israeli community, contributing to the cosmopolitan mosaic of the city, where one can find Americans, Russians, Ethiopians, Eritreans, South Africans, and more. Tel Aviv has a thriving gay community (25% of the city identifies as LGBT) and hosts the largest Pride Parade in the Middle East.[64] The second largest, and the only other Pride Parade in the Middle East is held in Jerusalem.

HAIFA

Haifa is one of the most unique cities in Israel, as its demographics are split between Jews and Arabs and therefore, the city reflects both cultures in a true model of co-existence.[65] The "capital of the North," Haifa boasts beautiful mountain views, an eclectic food scene, and one of the biggest Christmas celebrations in Israel. Haifa is also home to the Technion, one of Israel's most prestigious universities. A common saying among Israelis is, "We work in Haifa, pray in Jerusalem, and play in Tel Aviv." Haifa is also the official headquarters of the Baha'i faith, a relatively new belief system established in Iran in the 19th century. Followers believe in the goodwill and unity between all people and all religions, and after being expelled from Iran, they established the magnificent Baha'i gardens and a temple in Haifa, a place now open for all Israelis and tourists from around the world to enjoy. [66]

KIBBUTZIM AND MOSHAVIM

Kibbutzim and Moshavim (singular: **kibbutz** and **moshav**) are agricultural communities usually found near Israel's borders, notably in the north by the Syrian and Lebanese borders and in the south by the borders of Jordan and Egypt. Kibbutzim are structured around socialist and communitarian ideas, meaning many of them divide work between the members and distribute income equally (though many have allowed the free market to intrude just a little). Kibbutzim also have bragging rights for disproportionately contributing to Israel's innovation, defense, and culture. The Kibbutzim along the **Gaza** border are known for being the most peace-loving and humanitarian communities; nevertheless, Kibbutz Be'eri along with K'far Aza and Nir Oz were invaded on October 7th, 2023 and saw their residents massacred, raped, and kidnapped by **Hamas** (more on that later).

THE NEGEV

In the south of Israel lies a vast desert, the **Negev**, which once was an arid and only sparsely populated spot, but now represents something of a miracle in innovation and ingenuity. Not only is the Negev home to bustling cities, such as Be'er Sheva, Eilat, Asdod, and Ashkelon, but also to many small communities and kibbutzim who use cutting-edge technology to access resources like water and energy. The Negev is also home to the **Bedouin**, a migratory population of Muslims who have fought in recent years to receive more recognition from Israeli society and government.

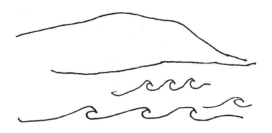

THE GALILEE AND THE GOLAN

In the north of the country lies the **Sea of Galilee** and the **Golan Heights**, one of the most beautiful regions in the entire country, and culturally significant to Jews, Muslims, and Christians (the sea is where Christians believe Jesus Christ walked on water). The area, like most of the north, is divided roughly evenly between Muslims and Jews, and hosts important cities such as Tiberias, a Jewish city well-recorded in ancient times, and **Safed** (also known as **Tzvat**), the center of Jewish mysticism as of centuries ago and home to Israeli artist colonies and spiritual devotion.[67] In 1981, Israel officially declared the Golan Heights as sovereign Israeli territory. Note, this territory is of strategic importance, as the Golan had been used by Syrians to attack Israeli civilians since the founding of the state. The United States recognized Israel's sovereignty in 2019.[68]

INNOVATION

One of the mission statements of Israel, found in its Declaration of Independence, is to be "the light unto the nations," that is, to produce ideas and things that benefit not just Israelis and Jews, but all of humanity. Israelis have lived up to this ideal through *innovation* – creating something out of nothing, as seen in its unique contributions and characteristics that people the world over continue to marvel at. These include but are not limited to...

Hebrew

One of the most (if not *the most*) astounding accomplishments of the Jewish people is the revival of Hebrew. Previously associated exclusively with prayer and rabbinic study, Hebrew is now the official language of the modern state of Israel, and spoken by nine million people, not only in Israel.[69] Many hardworking scholars contributed to the re-launching of Hebrew using ancient texts, but most prominent among them is **Eliezer Ben Yehuda (1858-1922)**, who styled the first modern Hebrew dictionary, and, as legend has it, forced his children to speak nothing but Hebrew at the expense of their mental health and social lives.[70] Ben Yehuda is seen as the father of modern Hebrew, and without his and his family's work, it would hardly have been possible to resuscitate a Jewish national identity, strong and cohesive enough to unite all different types of Jews under a single flag.

Tech

You've heard of "Silicon Valley," but have you heard of Silicon Wadi? Silicon Wadi refers to the Israeli tech industry that achieved success in the late 20th century. Israel's success in tech, inventions like facial recognition and SodaStream, combined with companies like Waze and Wix, has earned it the name the "start-up nation."[71] When living in a place like Tel Aviv, it is common to know at least ten people working in tech.

Cuisine

The Mediterranean palette is known as one of the healthiest in the world, and while In Israel you can definitely find your fair share of tomatoes, olives, and feta cheese, you can also find Yemeni, Ethiopian, Arabic, French, and even American food all around the same street corner in a place like Tel Aviv or Jerusalem. Many people say that to get to the more authentic scene, however, heading to small towns and villages deep within Israel are the best. A staple of Israeli cuisine, invented by an Iraqi Jew, is *sabich*, a combination of vegetables and egg in a warm and delicious pita. Tel Aviv also has one of the highest populations of vegan restaurants per capita in the world.[72] Israeli chefs like Yotam Ottolenghi and Eyal Shani have imported a fusion of Middle Eastern, Eastern European, and Mediterranean cuisine to cities all over the world.

Art and Architecture

Jerusalem is famous for its light limestone, called "Jerusalem Stone," mined from the hills near the city since antiquity. In the heart of Tel Aviv lies a **UNESCO** Heritage Site called "Ha'ir Lavan," the White City, named for a unique style of architecture called **Bauhaus**.[73] The Bauhaus architects fled Germany at the beginning of the Nazi era, accused of creating "degenerate art," but found fertile soil for their creativity in the rising Jewish state. Tel Aviv is known for its Bauhaus-style buildings, and Israel at-large is known for its own national style of art as well, influenced by American comics, Soviet aesthetics, and Middle Eastern traditions.

GOVERNMENT

Since its birth in 1948, Israel has remained a vibrant, multiracial, pluralistic democracy. Many other states born around the same time have fallen into a form of authoritarianism since, such as Pakistan, South Africa, Sudan, Lebanon, and Vietnam. However, Israel, throughout repeated existential wars, terrorism, political assassinations, and periods of social unrest and occupation, has remained a democratic state. Why? Because the Jewish people are accustomed to arguments and disagreements with each other – it is an integral part of the culture. Therefore, a functioning Israel state means listening to as many points of view as possible, including those of its Arab population.

DAVID BEN-GURION

Meet **David Ben-Gurion**, the first Prime Minister of Israel who served from 1948 to 54, and 1955 to 63. He is known as the "architect of the state" by Israelis and is the namesake of Israel's main international airport. Ben-Gurion was born in Plonsk, Ukraine, as David *Grun* in 1886. He emigrated to Ottoman Palestine in 1906 to work on a kibbutz. In 1909, as it was common for new immigrants to *Hebraicize* their names, he adopted the name "Ben-Gurion," after a fabled warrior of the Jewish-Roman war. Ben-Gurion quickly rose through the ranks of leadership in the pre-state Jewish community, called the **Yishuv**. He was the preeminent leader of the Yishuv during the British Mandate over Palestine and by 1948, he was the obvious choice for Prime Minister of the new state, especially after being the man to officially declare Israel's independence.

The Knesset

The center of power in Israel is the **Knesset**, the equivalent of a parliament. Parliamentary systems are the most common form of successful, long-standing democracies, and Israel's is no exception. The Knesset is made up of 120 members, divided into various parties that change nearly every election cycle.[74] The parties represent the many different streams in Israeli society: religious, secular, Sephardi, Ashkenazi, Russian, Ethiopian, right, left, center, and more. Israel is known for its consistent elections (sometimes a little too consistent) to decide the balance of power in the Knesset, shaped by proportional representation. This means that the number of votes a party receives from the public translates to how many seats in parliament they are awarded.

The Supreme Court & Basic Laws

Like most democracies, Israel has a Supreme Court, which has jurisdiction over all lower courts. The 15 judges of the court are chosen by a judicial selection committee and have the power to review and veto laws passed by the Knesset.[75] Israel currently does not have a constitution. Instead it has a series of laws called **basic laws**, which the Supreme Court decided in the 1990s could be judged as legally binding – essentially constitutional.[76] There are many basic laws, such as the law of human dignity and liberty which protects freedom of religion and freedom of expression to all citizens of Israel, and the nation-state law, which explicitly defines Israel as the nation-state of the Jewish people.

The 2023 Democracy Protests

After the swearing in of Israel's current government in late 2022, its ministers made public plans to curtail the powers of the Supreme Court. Many citizens who voted for the opposition viewed the "judicial overhaul" as a plan by the right-wing and religious parties to capitalize on their power. The country saw nearly 40 straight weeks of street protests and strikes in 2023, which ended with the existential crisis posed by the October 7th Massacre of 2023.[77]

BENJAMIN NETANYAHU

Benjamin Netanyahu is the longest serving Prime Minister of Israel, having first been elected to office in 1996.[78] After serving in the Sayeret Matkal, an elite unit in the Israeli Defense Forces, Netanyhau began his political career in America, advocating for Israel on mainstream media channels. His leadership in Israel has been both controversial and critical. Supporters of Netanyahu point to the expansion of the Israeli economy, the building of the "Start-Up Nation," the signing of peace deals with Arab nations resulting in the **Abraham Accords** in 2020, and a relative, if unwarranted, feeling of safety among Israeli citizens until 2023. Those critical of Netanyahu point to his indictment on corruption and bribery charges by Israel's Attorney General, the increasingly fraught divisions in Israeli society, and of course, the October 7th Massacre of 2023, which occurred under his watch.[79]

THE MILITARY

Every Jewish Israeli, both men and women, apart from members of the Haredi community (a source of major controversy in Israel), is drafted into the Israeli Defense Forces (IDF) at the age of 18 for at least two years. There are many different forces within the IDF, from the elite **Sayeret Matkal** unit that operates in combat zones, to the tank brigades, to intelligence, to the IDF Spokesperson Unit: the communications department. Service in the army is a formative experience for many Israelis, as it combines many sectors of Israeli society and inspires a sense of unity. The heads of the security forces are big players in government decision-making, especially during wartime.

The IDF takes extensive precautions when engaged in combat and operates with a level of transparency unmatched by any other army in the world. The military routinely releases footage of personnel calling off airstrikes on Gaza terrorist sites when civilians are seen in the area, they have a strict protocol for when to fire weapons, and if a soldier violates such protocols, he or she can serve time in prison. IDF lawyers who operate outside the army's chain of command independently review each airstrike.[80] When striking a military site near civilian buildings, the IDF takes every measure not to harm noncombatants by dropping leaflets in the area, urging building owners to tell residents to evacuate in Arabic.[81] The IDF even developed a special practice called "roof knocking" wherein they drop a non-explosive device which causes a bang encouraging any remaining people to leave, followed by a warning shot."[82] In contrast, both Hamas and Islamic Jihad, armed groups in the Gaza Strip which we will discuss at length in later chapters, have used the IDF's high standard of ethics against Israel. Terrorists send civilians to rooftops when Israel has warned of an airstrike, plant weapons caches in civilian areas, and use mosques and schools as a headquarters for militant activity.[83]

The Iron Dome

One of the most incredible feats of innovation developed by Israel in a partnership with the United States is the **Iron Dome**. Because Israel has had tens of thousands of rockets fired at its citizens from hostile armies on its borders, Israel developed cutting-edge missile defense technology to protect its civilians. To be absolutely clear, the Iron Dome does not shoot rockets at other people or countries. Instead, it intercepts rockets sent to harm Israel mid-air, saving the lives of countless civilians.[84] You might have heard about various U.S. Congress members trying to stop the funding of this critical defense system – which would be lethal.

MODERN ISRAEL: LAND, WARS, AND TREATIES IN 60 SECONDS

1800s Early Migration

Jews begin moving to Palestine, controlled by the Ottoman Empire, to establish communal farming communities and a center of Jewish life outside the city of Jaffa (later known as Yafo in Hebrew,) later developing methods of self-defense. At this time, Jerusalem has a majority Jewish population.

1917 World War I

The Ottoman Empire collapses and the British take control over "Mandatory Palestine." Lord Balfour of Britain pens the "Balfour Declaration," pledging support for a Jewish national home in Palestine. Jewish immigration continues apace.

1939 - 1945 World War II

Due to growing pressure and violence from Arabs, Britain places strict prohibitions on Jewish emigration to Palestine. When it becomes clear how many Jews are being killed in Europe, people all over the world become galvanized for the creation of a Jewish state.

1947 United Nations Vote

After the defeat of the Nazis and the establishment of the United Nations, on November 29, 1947, the UN votes to partition Palestine into a Jewish and Arab state.

1948 War of Independence

At the expiration of the British Mandate over Palestine, Israel declares independence. 7 Arab armies invade the new state, but Israel emerges victorious. At this time, approximately 750,000 Arab Palestinians flee the ensuing fighting between Israel and the Arab states on their own accord, or are compelled to leave by Arab leaders, or are expelled by the new Israeli forces. This becomes known as the **Nakba**, Arabic for catastrophe, a word coined by Syrian intellectual Constantin Zeuriq (to denote the humiliation experienced after the defeat of the 7 Arab armies at the hands of the Jews – more on this later.)

1967 Six Day War

Jordan, Egypt, and Syria launch a war to try again to annihilate the state of Israel. But against the odds, the Israelis win the war. At the end of fighting, Israel holds the new territories of the **West Bank** and East Jerusalem from Jordan, Gaza and the **Sinai Peninsula** from Egypt, and the **Golan Heights** from Syria.

1973 Yom Kippur War

Syria and Egypt again invade Israel, beginning a devastating conflict.

1978 Peace Treaty with Egypt

President **Anwar Sadat** and Prime Minister **Menachem Begin** come to the table and reach an agreement. Israel gives the Sinai Peninsula back to Egypt.

1988-1991 First Intifada
Intifada means violent uprising or literally "shaking off," and specifically denotes campaigns of terror against Israeli civilians by Palestinians. The First Intifada begins as protests against the Israeli occupation of the West Bank and Gaza, but spirals into a violent uprising in Israel proper, wherein innocent civilians are killed.

1993 Oslo Accords
In the early '90s, many Israelis believe that the "land for peace" formula, establishing Palestinian sovereignty in the West Bank and Gaza, would lead to peace. Talks begin with the Americans and **Yasser Arafat** to create the Palestinian Authority and discuss partition of the land.

1995 Assasination of Yitzhak Rabin
Prime Minister **Yitzhak Rabin**, who presided over the peace process, is assassinated by far-right Israeli, **Yigal Amir**.

2000 Camp David Summit
Prime Minister **Ehud Barak**, Palestinian Leader Yasser Arafat, and President Clinton convene in Maryland in 2000, where Palestinians are offered a state in the Gaza Strip and 95% of the West Bank.

2001-2005 Second Intifada
After the offer, Palestinians launch a bloody campaign of terrorism against Israelis to further derail the peace process, including bombing a Passover seder with Holocaust survivors in Netanya, a night-club full of teenagers in Tel Aviv, a pizzeria in Jerusalem with women and children including pregnant women, and a restaurant in Haifa with Muslims, Druze, and Jews. Over 1,000 Israelis are killed in the attacks.

2005-2006 Israel Withdraws from Gaza
Israel withdraws from the Gaza Strip which uproots hundreds of homes and thousands of Jewish citizens. **Hamas**, the terrorist organization, is elected to rule over Gaza soon after.

2006 - 2021 A Low Grade Terror Fever
Periodic rocket fire from Gaza into Israel and skirmishes in the Occupied Territories.

2020 The Abraham Accords
Named after the patriarch of the three major Abrahamic religions, Judaism, Christianity and Islam, The Abraham Accords, brokered by the United States, creates an historic alliance between Israel, the UAE, Bahrain and Sudan, with Morocco following soon after.

2023 October 7th Massacre and Beyond
On Oct 7th, from Gaza, Hamas invades Israel and massacres 1,200 people, taking over 200 people hostage, including women and children. **Hezbollah** in Lebanon continuously sends rockets into Israel starting the day after. Israel declares war and the IDF enters Gaza, discovers and destroys suspected tunnel networks and weakens Hamas. In 2024 Israel enters Lebanon, and weakens Hezbollah. In April 2024, Iran launches missiles at Israel directly for the first time and Israel then takes out Iran's capabilities for future attacks via airstrikes. The power centers in the Middle East shift once again.

Z IS FOR ZIONISM

The Hebrew Bible refers to the land of Israel and Jerusalem as Zion. Several hundreds of years ago, those involved in the movement to reestablish the Jewish homeland and right to self-determination adopted the name, symbolizing the connection to the land that was integral to the Jewish people. Today, the words *Zionism* and *Zionist* are demonized quite often by those who consider themselves progressive. But Zionism is in actuality quite the opposite: is it the Jewish civil rights movement, entirely in line with human rights and the freedom of historically oppressed peoples. The movement of "**anti-Zionism**," which in the modern era refers to the dismantling of the world's only Jewish state, by contrast, is by very nature regressive.

Origins of Zionism

The Jewish people are a nation – a population of people united by common ancestry, language, culture, land, and religion. Many credit the Jewish people with introducing the concept of a nation to the world, and with it, the modern idea of self-determination, which simply means that the people of a nation get to decide their future for themselves.[85] During the 18th and 19th centuries, empires, who ruled over the majority of the earth from the British to the Ottomans, routinely clashed over borders and resources. Individual peoples, including the Egyptians, Ukrainians, Czechs, Poles, Fins, Syrians, Armenians, and Kurds, began to resist subjugation by imperialist rule and demanded countries of their own.

The Jews, scattered across the world, did not form a sustainable majority capable of self-defense anywhere. Even when European countries emancipated their Jews, granting

Origins of Zionism *(cont.)*

them equal civil rights, the lack of a Jewish state meant that other states routinely inflicted violence upon Jewish communities as an outlet for their own problems. The Jews were the "no-fail" target of any group or ruler who wished to pinpoint a group as a scapegoat for a failure, as there was little the Jews could do to defend themselves or inflict damage on their enemies.

At the same time that empires were falling, murmurs about returning to Zion were becoming louder amongst the Jews from every corner. Books such as "Rome and Jerusalem" by Moses Hesse (1862), and "Discourse on the Restoration of the Jews" by Mordechai Noah (1844), started to appear in Europe and America, respectively.

TO THE BIRD

...Sing, my bird, of the wonders of the land
Spring is coming, but to stay forever.
Will you bring me from the bounty of the land,
From the valleys and ravines, from the mountaintops? Has God
had compassion, has he comforted Zion,
Or is she still left to the graves?
...Does the dew drip like pearls on Mount Hermon Does it drip
and fall like tears?
....O that I had wings to fly to the land
    - Excerpt from *To the Bird* by Russian poet **H.N. Bialik** in 1891

The Jewish State by Theodor Herzl

One of the most significant books for the Jewish people is a small, 100 page pamphlet by playwright, lawyer, and journalist **Theodor Herzl**, called *Der Judenstaat, The Jewish State*, in English. Published in 1896 to great controversy in Europe and in the Jewish world, it is credited with launching the Zionist movement in its modern political form.

In *The Jewish State*, Herzl calls for a mass exodus of Jews from Europe, predicting imminent disaster, and encourages the establishment of an independent Jewish state in the Jewish ancient homeland of what was then called Palestine.[86] Herzl describes in great detail the political, financial, and logistical means of accomplishing the goals of Zionism, but also the spiritual and religious significance in such an undertaking as well.

The Jewish State concludes with:

> *Therefore I believe that a wondrous generation of Jews will spring into existence. The Maccabees will rise again. Let me repeat once more my opening words: The Jews who wish for a State will*

have it. We shall live at last as free men on our own soil, and die peacefully in our own homes. The world will be freed by our liberty, enriched by our wealth, magnified by our greatness.[87]

Herzl Awakens A People

After The Jewish State's publication and undeniable popularity, Herzl worked tirelessly for several years across Europe, eventually organizing the **First Zionist Congress** in Basel, Switzerland in 1897. Throngs of Jews gathered in Basel to exchange ideas on the possibility of establishing an independent Jewish country. Shortly after the congress, Herzl wrote in his diary: *"At Basel I founded the Jewish State. If I said this out loud today, I would be greeted by universal laughter. In five years perhaps, and certainly in fifty years, everyone will perceive it."*[88] Fifty-one years after Herzl penned these words, David Ben-Gurion declared the new, independent State of Israel in Tel Aviv, in front of a large portrait of Theodor Herzl, who is still recognized today as the founder of the country.

Herzl went on to write another important book before his early death, **Altneuland**, a futuristic utopian novel which describes the Jewish state after Zionism had succeeded. Not only are the Jews finally free and equal with all nations of the world in *Altneuland*, but their country boasts progressive achievements including suffrage for women, religious and racial equality, democracy, workers rights, and even environmentalism. So much of what Herzl wrote has come to fruition. Zionist congresses continue to this day, long after Herzl's death in 1904.

THE DREYFUS AFFAIR

Herzl initially believed that assimilation was the primary method of ensuring safety for the Jews of Europe, until two profound historical developments occurred. As a journalist, Herzl reported on the Dreyfus Trial, or as it is better known now, the **Dreyfus Affair**, the proceedings against Captain **Alfred Dreyfus** of the French Army. Dreyfus, possibly the most assimilated and nationalistic a Jew could become in Europe, was falsely accused of relaying French military secrets to the German army, also known as treason. He was sent to a prison in a French penal colony, where he endured miserable conditions for over five years. In seeing the effect of the trial on the French, including viewing a throng of citizens crying *"Death to the Jews!"* outside the courthouse, Herzl reached the conclusion that European emancipation had failed, and that another solution to the Jewish question was needed. Soon after the Dreyfus Affair, Karl Lueger was elected Mayor of Vienna in 1897. Lueger, a vicious antisemite, had unleashed a flurry of hatred in Austria, which many say was the ideological precursor to Hitler's Nazism. Herzl knew that the time to act was *now.*[89]

DIFFERENT FORMS OF ZIONISM

Zionism is not one idea. Far from it. Because of how true the cliche of "Two Jews, three opinions" is, Zionism at its birth and to this day comes in many different flavors. The foundation of all Zionisms is belief in the establishment of a Jewish state in the Land of Israel, but Zionists find a way to argue over everything from borders, to economics, religion, foreign policy, and more. These differences of opinion often form the political divides in Israeli society and even among Jews in the Diaspora.

Religious Zionism
Herzl's Zionism was fundamentally secular in nature, but in the centuries leading up to his emergence as a Jewish leader, religious Jews from Europe to the Middle East passionately encouraged their devout followers to move to Palestinian cities like Tzvat and Jerusalem to renew a spiritual Jewish life in the Holy Land[90]. Among them were Rabbi Zvi Hirsch Kalischer, Rabbi Moshe Shmuel Glasner, and Rabbi Abraham Isaac Kook. Safed became known as the center of *Kabbalah*, or Jewish mysticism, by as early as the 16th century, inhabited by important wise men like Rabbi Yaakov bi Rav and Rabbi Moses ben Jacob. Today, Religious Zionists continue to believe that settling the land of Israel is a commandment from God that will hasten the coming of the Jewish Messiah.

Socialist/Labor Zionism

Around the time that Herzl penned *The Jewish State*, Jews were arriving in Palestine and building new communities called kibbutzim.[91] The idea behind kibbutzim was Jewish national renewal, grounded in socialist economic principles, strong ties to the Land of Israel, secularism, and modern Hebrew. Socialist/labor Zionists believed that by "working the land" and creating a new society, Jews would be inspired to break free of their antisemitic host countries, and the world would be inspired toward socialist revolution. The kibbutzim were widely successful in not only building an economy and a political system in pre-state Israel, but also in establishing units of self-defense for Jewish communities and an infrastructure to absorb Jewish immigrants.

Zionism Today

Today, Zionism is expressed by the existence and the protection of the state of Israel. Zionism is a force that spans both sides of the political spectrum and every type of religiosity from secular to orthodox. Even Christians and Muslims believe in and fight for Israel's and the Jews' rights to self-determination. Zionism is ultimately a **Jewish civil rights movement**, where Jews are freed from their centuries-long status of oppression and subjugation from other nations. Zionism guarantees the Jewish people a method of defense to prevent further violence and discrimination and also grants Jews a seat at the table of international affairs. Zionism allows Jews to authentically live out the customs of their ancestors, and for the modern Jewish culture to flourish and evolve.

עַם יִשְׂרָאֵל חַי

Am Yisrael Chai

The best way to understand and appreciate Zionism is to experience it oneself. There is no place like Israel in the world. The country is filled with beautiful and patriotic citizens of every shade of skin, religion, ideological creed, and value system. When people come to the Jewish state for the first time, especially those who have been heavily indoctrinated with an entirely different and negative picture, they often become the biggest Zionists. All the cultures, cuisines, and fashions coalesce into a vibrating energy, unparalleled in any other country, flipping on its head the traditional understanding of who the Jewish people are. Book a flight and see it for yourself!

3

THE NEIGHBORHOOD

The Middle East is known for its spices, cuisine, rugs...and wars. The region is composed of dozens, if not hundreds, of different peoples, religions, languages, and cultures, a diverse mosaic, but the region's history of conquests, expulsions, and even genocides have made surviving as "different" extraordinarily difficult. The greatest event that shaped the Middle East was the **Muslim conquest** of the 7th and 8th centuries, right after Islam was born. Islam claimed by force an enormous slice of the world, including North Africa, Asia, and parts of Europe, and subjugated all non-Muslims to second-class citizens (if they were lucky enough to hang onto their unique way of life at all). This is why the Middle Eastern world today remains overwhelmingly Muslim.

THE ISLAMIC CONQUEST OF THE MIDDLE EAST

Today, due to the Muslim conquests, which erased countless indigenous cultures and, in some cases, peoples, there are over 50 Muslim majority countries and authoritative Muslim institutions.[92] 99.6% of the land in the Middle East is majority Muslim.

Understanding Islam: Sunni vs. Shia
Sunni Muslims and **Shiite Muslims** (also known as Shia Muslims) make up the two major sects of Islam. After the Islamic Prophet Mohammed died in 632 C.E., there was disagreement as to who should become the *caliph*, or religious heir/ruler. Some thought he should be chosen by the people, others that he should be a descendant of Mohammed. Those who believed the heir should be a descendant came to be known as "Shiites," and those who believed the heir should be chosen by the people became known as Sunnis.These two groups are historically enemies with bitter and bloody rivalries fought between them for hundreds of years that continue into today's conflicts.[93]

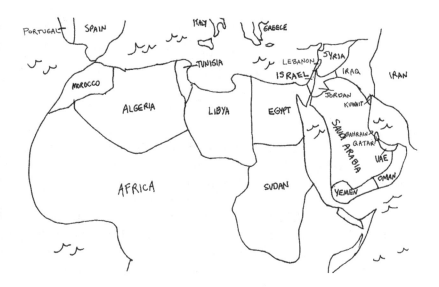

PRESENT DAY MIDDLE EASTERN NATIONS

Iran

Iran was a center of culture and regional power for centuries, the capital of empire and civilization. Iran has always had a special relationship with the Jewish people from the time of Cyrus the Great, the ancient Babylonian king who allowed the Jews to return to Jerusalem and rebuild the Second Temple.[94] Much later, Iran was one of the first Muslim majority countries to recognize the State of Israel (de-facto) in the 1950s.[95] This is the legacy of Iran-Israel relations and a part of Persian culture that is cherished by many Iranians today. In 1979, foreign interference coupled with an alliance of communists and Islamists – including Palestinian terrorist organizations in Lebanon – led to the overthrow of the Iranian monarchy. When the dust settled and the **Shah** (king) escaped into exile, power was concentrated by one man: **Ayatollah** (meaning *religious leader*) **Khomeini**, who turned Iran into a totalitarian Shiite **theocracy**.

Iran *(cont.)*

Personal liberties were drastically curtailed. Women were required to conceal themselves in public.[96] Mass executions of supporters of the Shah began. Regime officials carried out unprecedented barbarism, some even publicly executing their own children.[97] Public life was placed under the watch of a religiously zealous police state. Foreign policy, beyond a broad rejection of Western values, centered around loathing of the United States (called "the Great Satan") and, more immediately, Israel (called "the Little Satan").

Since the revolution, the **Islamic Republic** has become the prime exporter of Islamist terrorism against both "satans," sponsoring and providing funding, training, and weapons to Israel's neighboring enemies: Hezbollah in Lebanon, Hamas and **Islamic Jihad** in Gaza, the **Houthis** in Yemen, **Kataib Hezbollah** in Iraq, and other **Islamic Revolutionary Guard Corps** (IRGC)-affiliated terror groups in Syria. The regime's explicit goal is to destroy the State of Israel in its entirety.[98] They have even put a countdown clock to "Israel's destruction" in the capital city of Tehran.[99] Iran has caused immeasurable destabilization and suffering throughout the entire region, creating and financing devastating civil wars in Lebanon, Syria, Iraq, and Yemen.[100]

The majority of Iran's own people despise the leadership of the Islamic Republic regime despite being a Muslim majority country.[101] There have been repeated attempts to overthrow the regime. Recently, supporting Israel has become a core value for the people of Iran as a statement of rejection of the pro-terror values of the regime. On a regular basis, videos can be found circulating on social media showing Iranians refusing to walk on the American and Israeli flags which the regime places outside schools in the country.[102]

IRAN'S TERROR OCTOPUS

Throughout the last few decades, sometimes as a slow crescendo and other times with a bang, Israel has needed to repeatedly defend itself from its neighbors in the form of "proxy wars," most often instigated or funded by the Islamic Republic of Iran. A **proxy war** is when another country is controlling or encouraging an attack towards its target through a country other than its own. Envision Iran as the head of an octopus, thrashing its tentacles in the form of Hamas, Hezbollah, the Houthis, and Palestinian Islamic Jihad. Only in April of 2024 did the Islamic Republic directly attack Israel for the first time, shooting over three-hundred rockets, drones, and missiles into Israel airspace, all of which were shut down by the Israeli Air Force and surrounding nations.

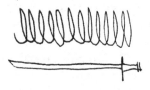

Saudi Arabia

Saudi Arabia is home to **Mecca**, the holiest site for the entire Muslim faith. Muslims from all over the world take part in the *Hajj*, or pilgrimage, at least once in their life as mandated by the Qur'an and holy teachings. Saudi Arabia is ruled virtually completely by a very wealthy and powerful Sunni royal family, currently headed by **Crown Prince Muhamed Bin Salman**, or as he is more commonly known, MBS. MBS is credited with bringing comparatively liberal reforms to the country, such as the incremental easing of restrictions on women, but by and large, Saudi Arabia remains an undemocratic and authoritarian society, with repression against speech, human rights, religion, and press,[103] although slow shifts appear to be underway.[104] Relations between Saudi Arabia and the U.S. tend to oscillate based on U.S. dependence on foreign oil markets and, of late, relations between Saudi Arabia and Israel have thawed from cool to medium. Many in the Middle East and around the world today wonder if further conflict between Saudi Arabia and the Islamic Republic of Iran, the leaders of the Sunni and Shiite worlds, respectively, will give way to an agreement to eventually normalize relations between the Saudis and Israelis.

Egypt

Egypt holds a uniquely important place in Jewish history. It is the land from which the Jews fled to Israel thousands of years ago, the story recited every Passover holiday. It is also the opening of the Ten Commandments: *"I am the Lord your God, who brought you out of the land of Egypt, out of the house of slavery; you shall have no other gods before me."*[105] After that Kingdom of Ancient Egypt was conquered by Alexander the Great in 332 B.C.E, it later succumbed to Islam in 641 C.E., and in the modern era, was a part of the Ottoman Empire until established as a British Protectorate at the time of the founding of Israel.

In 1952, the Egyptian military overthrew the monarchy that had operated under Britain, and installed itself as the governing body of the Egyptian people.[106] Egypt was once a thriving developing nation with a large Jewish population, but with the rise of the virulently anti-Israel new Egyptian regime, and later the **Muslim Brotherhood** and political Islam, the country and its attitude toward Jews rapidly deteriorated. Egyptians have only experienced about two years of non-autocratic rule since 1952. The first authoritarian leader was **General Gamal Abdel Nasser**, whose brand of **Arab nationalism** called for death to the Jews and Israel in 1967, repeated by Anwar El-Sadat in 1973. However, in 1977, Sadat changed his tone, and made "cold peace" (recognition of the nation, a cease in hostilities), with Israel, which continues to this day.[107] Egypt is the only country other than Israel to share a border with the Gaza Strip.

THE BEN EZRA SYNAGOGUE, CAIRO

Egypt recently restored the famous Ben Ezra Synagogue, although without enough Jews for even a **minyan** (a quorum of ten Jewish men), it operates as a tourist destination rather than a synagogue. Why so few Jews? One reason: after World War II, a high-ranking Nazi official named Johann Von Leers fled to Egypt, converted to Islam, and took the name **Omar Amin**. In Germany, Von Leers had worked with Josef Goebbels, Hitler's Chief Propagandist, to craft the messaging which contributed to the killing of 6 million Jews. In Egypt, he brought his Nazi ideology and messaging skills with him to the Middle East which contributed to the expulsion of all 80,000 Jews from Egypt between World War II and 1967.[108]

Lebanon

Lebanon, a formerly majority Christian country which is now majority Muslim, borders the northern part of Israel.[109] Its capital of Beirut was once considered the "Paris of the Middle East" before Palestinian terrorists settled and took hold in the 1970s. This ultimately contributed to plunging Lebanon into a civil war. Lebanon has a long history of conflict with large populations of different Shia and Sunni Muslims as well as Christians. Today, the Islamic Republic of Iran dominates via their proxy terror group, Hezbollah, formed in the 1980s.[110] The Islamic Republic's interference and occupation of Lebanon has caused tremendous damage to the country, destroying its economy and state institutions.[111] Destabilization is a core strategy of the Islamic Republic for expanding influence. A weak society is a society that can be more easily controlled (see *Lebanon, Hezbollah,* and *Exploding Beepers* later in this chapter).

LEBANON

Syria

Syria is a country rich in culture and peoplehood, but has experienced great political instability. Since the end of World War II, there has been a nearly constant tug-of-war for power in Syria between socialists, Islamists, moderates, and nationalists. Since the 1990s, the Ba'ath Party dominates Syria, a socialist/ Arab nationalist party (with Nazi-inspired antisemitism added to the mix) led by President **Bashar al-Assad**. 2011 saw the beginning of the Syrian Civil War, during which Assad, backed by the Islamic Republic, Hezbollah, and Russia, fought against both Sunni opposition militias, the **Kurdish people** (an ethnic minority in the Middle East sharing many political similarities with Jews,) and Islamist terror organizations like **ISIS**. The war left more than 300,000 civilians dead, including over 4,000 Palestinians.[112] Syria fought against Israel in 1948, 1967, and 1973. In 1967, they lost control of the mountainous Golan Heights region. After the IDF degraded Hezbollah's strength in response to their attacks after the October 7th Massacre, rebel factions seized control of the country. Assad fled to Russia, opening a power vacuum. The future of Syria is uncertain.

THE MUSLIM BROTHERHOOD

In 1928, an Egyptian school teacher named Hassan Al Banna founded an Islamic political ideology called the Muslim Brotherhood which promotes a more aggressive and radical interpretation of Islamic traditions and values through preaching and social welfare.[113] The organization plays an active role in the politics of many Arab nations today, and has set up many organizations, including the **Muslim Student Association** (MSA), which are prevalent at American universities. The Muslim Brotherhood has been banned and designated as a terrorist organization in Egypt, Saudi Arabia, and the UAE.[114] In Egypt, The Muslim Brotherhood took over the country during the **Arab Spring**, a series of rebellions against dictators across the Middle East that took place in the early 2010s. The Muslim Brotherhood tried to change the constitution to their own liking, prompting a coup by the Egyptian military, led by Abdel Fattah Al Sisi, who is now the head of state.

Jordan

The "Emirate of Transjordan" was established in 1921 by the British, when land formerly ruled by the Ottoman Empire was divided up by the Allied Powers after World War I. Britain awarded governance of the land to the **Hashemite** dynasty, a wealthy and powerful family from Saudi Arabia. Jordan claimed its independence from Britain in 1946, and soon after, declared war upon the new state of Israel, capturing the land west of the Jordan river (the "West Bank"), in the process.[115] Jordan is one of the smaller and more resource-poor states in the Middle East. It is home to two million Palestinians, numbering close to 60% of its population.[116] The kingdom seems weaker than its neighbors by almost every measure – politically, economically, militarily – yet curiously maintains more stability due to its long standing alliances with the United States, the UK, and the EU. Jordan has a technical peace treaty with Israel, though its rulers and population remain hostile.

Qatar

Qatar sits on the peninsula in the Persian Gulf and gained independence from Britain in 1971. Since then, it has been ruled by an absolute monarchy.[117] For such a small country, Qatar is fabulously rich, boasting the fourth highest GDP in the world, but this wealth is largely in the hands of very few people at the top. Most, if not all, labor in the country operates through an indentured workforce of migrants. Some consider this a form of modern day slavery (approximately 37 workers died while building the World Cup Stadium in Doha, Qatar's capital, in anticipation of hosting the World Cup in 2022).[118] In the 21st century, Qatar plays an outsized role in sponsoring Palestinian terrorist organizations, including Hamas.[119] Qatar also serves

Qatar *(cont.)*

as a "mediator" between the West and Islamist terror groups, and simultaneously provides a safe haven within their capital to leaders of terrorist organizations, including **Ismail Haniyeh** from Hamas, one of the key orchestrators of the October 7th Massacre. The United States maintains this cordiality due to having a major American military base on the island from which it conducts operations in the Middle East. The state-sponsored Qatari news agency, **Al-Jazeera**, broadcasts in English and Arabic, often with wildly different messages, and also spreads libels about Israel and the Jewish people. Some say it operates as a critical instrument for Muslim Brotherhood propaganda.

UAE

The United Arab Emirates (UAE) is a combination of seven Arab monarchies, called emirates, which together comprise one of the most wealthy countries in the region due to its abundant supply of oil. Abu Dhabi and Dubai, the two main cities of the UAE, are somewhat of an experiment in a more moderate form of Islam. Even though the royal family of the UAE exercises, still, near total power, and even though there exist very serious problems such as the mysterious disappearance of government critics and restrictions on freedom of religion, press, and association, the UAE has been drifting toward liberalization in recent years due to the growing negative influence of the Islamic Republic of Iran in the region.[120] Some of this liberalization was due to normalization with Israel in 2020, part of the momentous Abraham Accords. Since then, the UAE has built not only a synagogue in Dubai, but has also changed their country's textbooks to avoid antisemitic and anti-Israel tropes and has even built a Holocaust museum.[121]

Bahrain

Bahrain is a small nation off the coast of Saudi Arabia comprising fifty natural islands and thirty-three man-made islands. Bahrain declared independence from Britain as recently as 1971 and was declared an Islamic constitutional monarchy in 2002. Bahrain is considered a modern Arab state because of its valuable exports and bustling economy, and also because it signed onto the Abraham Accords in 2020 along with the United Arab Emirates, part of a growing alliance of Middle Eastern countries against the Islamic Republic of Iran, despite the fact that it has a sizable Shia Muslim population.[122]

Kuwait

Kuwait is a small country on the coast of the Persian Gulf which has known a history of violence, most notably, the 1990s Iraqi campaign led by Saddam Hussein to annex the country. The rulers of the kingdom of Kuwait have vast wealth which they dole out to citizens in an allowance. Kuwait today operates as an autocracy with most, if not all, power concentrated in the hands of the Emir, or monarch. Kuwait hosts the largest population of stateless people in the entire Middle East, which has made it a subject of a great deal of human rights criticism.[123]

Yemen

Yemen is a country to the direct south of Saudi Arabia – a place to which many Jews who now live in Israel trace back their ancestry. Unfortunately, because of decades of influence by the Islamic Republic of Iran and the brutal war in Yemen started by Islamic Republic proxy, the Houthis, almost no Jews remain in Yemen, and those who do live in constant fear of persecution. In 1949, Israel launched the famous **On Wings of Eagles** campaign, the airlifting of up to 50,000 Yemeni Jews and a few thousand from Saudi Arabia, Djibouti, and Eritrea.[124] The operation was named after a famous verse in the Bible: *"But those who wait for the Lord will gain new strength and renew their power; They will lift up their wings like eagles rising toward the sun. They will run and not become weary, They will walk and not grow tired."*[125]

Turkey

Modern Turkey emerged after the collapse of the **Ottoman Empire** at the end of World War I. After this, Turkey installed secular reforms: education systems, healthcare, a more trustworthy legal system; and rooted out the Muslim Brotherhood. But during World War II, Turkey declared itself as neutral and even profited from German Nazism.[126] Today, Turkey claims to be a democracy, although under President **Recyp Erdogan**'s rule, the country has suffered restrictions on freedom of speech, the press, assembly, and rights for minorities, including the LGBT community.[127] Over 20,000 intellectuals, teachers, and doctors have been imprisoned since 2015.[128] Turkey maintains a cool relationship with Israel, because, though the countries have never formally fought, Erdogan is known for his often troubling and even antisemitic statements.[129]

Morocco

Morocco, a country in North Africa which shares a border with Spain, saw a huge influx of Jewish refugees after Spain and Portugal expelled their Jews in the late 1400s. Many Jews both in Israel and around the world trace their ancestry back to Morocco, though today, the kingdom is home to only around 2,000. Sadly, Morocco was one of the countries to purge itself of its Jews after the establishment of Israel in 1948.[130] But there is hope. Though Morocco is ruled by a theocratic monarch like other Arab states in the region, in 2021, Israel and Morocco signed a series of agreements that normalized relations. The negotiations with Morocco, which followed the Abraham Accords with the UAE and Bahrain, inspired great optimism for the future of the Middle East.

Iraq

Like Morocco, Iraq boasted a rich tradition of Jewish culture. The Jewish community in Iraq traces back to the destruction of the First Temple and the exile to the Babylonian empire, today's modern Iraq. Before the establishment of Israel, they boasted more than 150,000 Jews in Iraq, the largest population of Jews in the Middle East, concentrated mainly in the bustling Jewish quarter of Baghdad. But beginning in 1941 with the *Farhud*, a violent pogrom against Iraq's Jews, the mass emigration to Israel began.[131] Today, according to the World Jewish Congress, there are only four Jews left in Iraq.[132] All the better: in the last thirty years, Iraq has undergone dictatorship, invasion, genocide, war, terrorism, and more war.

Afghanistan

Afghanistan is a mountainous country wedged between Iran and Pakistan, historically a coveted piece of land due to the large empires surrounding it. The Soviet Union invaded Afghanistan in 1979, killing approximately two million Afghanis in the process and installing a Marxist, anti-religious regime that was very unpopular with the public.[134] In 1994, the **Taliban**, a Sunni extremist organization dedicated to imposing **Sharia law** on the population, was established to combat oppressive conditions and poverty.[135] Within a few years, the Taliban had seized control

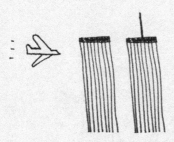

On **September 11, 2001**, an Islamic Terrorist Group named **Al Qaeda** used airplanes as weapons to fly into and destroy the Twin Towers of the World Trade Center and the Pentagon where over 3,000 people died in an invasion no less dramatic than the one on Israel on October 7, 2023, but far smaller relative to the U.S. population. In 2001, the U.S. invaded Afghanistan for harboring the Taliban who gave refuge to Al Qaeda's leader and orchestrator of 9/11, a terrorist named Osama Bin Laden. Then in 2003 the U.S. invaded Iraq for their alleged development of chemical weapons. At least 430,000 civilians died directly as a result of the wars and millions more as a result of the U.S. response.[133]

of the entire country, making Afghanistan a hotbed for human rights abuses such as political kidnappings, public executions, and severe repression of women.

The Taliban ruled Afghanistan until America's invasion of the country shortly after the September 11, 2001, attacks. However, the American-supported, moderate Afghan government was not strong enough to beat back the Islamic threats, and when the Biden Administration removed American soldiers from the country in 2021, the Taliban reclaimed power in a matter of hours. Today, the country remains a primary exporter of terrorism, anti-Western militantism, and antisemitism, and girls are no longer allowed to be educated past sixth grade or speak in public.[136]

GENDER APARTHEID IN THE MIDDLE EAST

A defining feature of countries where strict Islam is incorporated into the state apparatus is the erasure of women. In the 1970s, Iran, Afghanistan, Syria, and Lebanon boasted cosmopolitan cities where women could show their hair freely, go about their business without supervision of a man, and even wear skirts above their knees on occasion. However, since the hostile Islamic revolutions that erupted in the last few decades, women in many Middle Eastern countries are subjected to such human rights atrocities as genital mutilation, forced child marriage, domestic abuse, and even murder at the hands of a father, husband, or brother, called **honor killings**.[137]

Women in Iran and Afghanistan are required at minimum to wear a hijab, or head covering, and at the strictest a full body and face covering, under punishment of lashes, imprisonment, or even death. **Mahsa Amini** was a young Kurdish-Iranian woman living in Tehran, the capital of Iran, where she was arrested by the Islamic Regime's **Morality Police** for improperly wearing her hijab and then beaten to death. Condemnation of Amini's murder on social media led to a worldwide protest movement against the Islamic Republic called "Women. Life. Freedom," led by the women living within its oppressive gender apartheid system.[138]

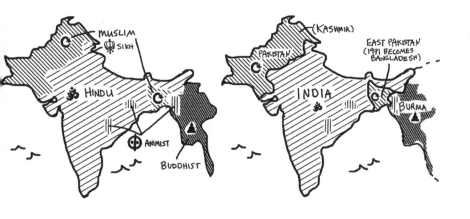

1909 BRITISH INDIAN EMPIRE   COUNTRIES FORMED AFTER WWII

India and Pakistan

India and Pakistan, as nation states, were also created in 1948 when the United Nations partitioned a great swath of land between two countries on the basis of peoplehood and religion. At least fourteen million people were displaced by the India-Pakistan partition, and at least one million were killed in the ensuing violence.[139] After the partition, India became 80% Hindu and 20% Muslim, with Pakistan standing at 97% Muslim.[140] India and Pakistan also have a disputed territory called Kashmir, with violent skirmishes from time to time over borders.[141] In 1992, after decades of anti-Israel policy, India signed a recognition agreement and relations with Israel have been increasingly warm since then with a high tourism exchange and common political interests against radical Islam.[142] Israel and Pakistan currently have no diplomatic relations.

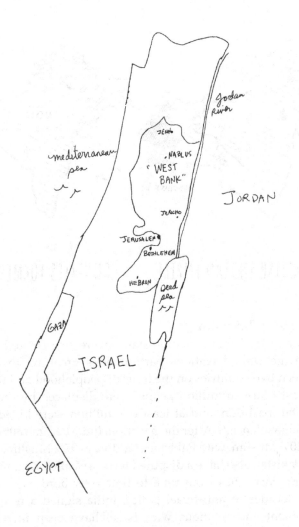

PALESTINIAN TERRITORIES

Historically, there has never been an independent Arab state of Palestine. Nevertheless, today, there are two major territories adjacent to Israel's borders designated as Palestinian.

The West Bank aka Judea and Samaria

The West Bank, called as such because it is a slice of land west of the Jordan River, comprises a variety of Palestinian majority cities including Ramallah, Nablus, Hebron, and Jenin, and smaller towns and villages including Masaffer, al-Bika'ia, and Huwara. The term The West Bank can be contentious (see below), but we will use The West Bank in this book. Many places in the West Bank, such as the ancient city of Jericho and the Old City of Hebron, are biblically significant to Jews and Christians. The West Bank includes Bethlehem, where Jesus Christ was born. Today, most population centers in the West Bank are governed by the Palestinian Authority under President **Mamhmoud Abbas** and the political party **Fatah**.

2000 B.C.E.   1948 A.D.

LANGUAGE IS IMPORTANT: THE "WEST BANK"

The term "The West Bank" was coined during the partition of 1947 west of the Jordan River. However, many Jews and the current government of Israel officially refer to the area by its biblical name, "Judea and Samaria" coined circa 2000 BCE. Use of the different names often reflects one's political leanings.

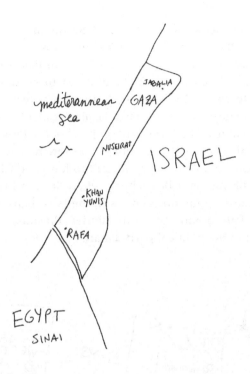

Gaza

Gaza, also known as the Gaza Strip, is a small piece of land on the Mediterranean Sea which borders Israel to its east and north and Egypt to its south. The population of Gaza stands at about 2 million people, a number that has grown significantly over the past several years.[143] Israelis pulled out of Gaza entirely in 2005, including exhuming graves of loved ones, and the Palestinians held the territory entirely. Since then, however, Gaza has been controlled entirely by the Palestinian terrorist organization Hamas, which has routinely launched wars against the State of Israel including in 2008, 2014, 2021, and 2023. We will discuss both the history of the Gaza Strip and Hamas at length in the next chapter.

THE 2023 OCTOBER 7TH MASSACRE

The October 7th Massacre of 2023, also known as "10/7," or in Israel as "Black Saturday," was the invasion of Israel's southern border by Palestinian civilians and Hamas militants from Gaza. The firing of thousands of rockets, aimed at civilians in dozens of Israeli cities, corresponded with the massacre of over 1,200 Israelis, and the taking of over 200 hostages: men, women, and children, from their homes and military bases into Hamas's underground tunnels.[144] October 7th is already seen as a defining moment in Israeli and Jewish history, the largest organized killing of Jews since the Holocaust.[145] This despicable, unforgivable attack involved the rape and mutilation of women, the kidnapping of children, torture, and a mass killing at the Nova music festival, and ended with overjoyed Palestinians passing candy out in the streets of Gaza and the West Bank.[146] In fact, many of the Hamas militants and civilian residents of Gaza livestreamed the brutality they inflicted on the kibbutzim along the Gaza border and the Nova musical festival, calling their relatives and friends to boast at how many Jews they had killed and/or kidnapped.[147] Many of Hamas's victims on October 7th were "peaceniks," devoted peace activists who helped in the transport of Gazans to Israeli hospitals for better medical treatment or to agricultural fields for better employment opportunities.

THE 2023 OCTOBER 7TH MASSACRE (CONT.)

The attacks on Israel have also continued from Yemen with attacks from the Houthis (a proxy of the Islamic regime in Iran), Iraq via proxies of the Islamic regime in Iran, and Syria via the Islamic Revolutionary Guard Corps and affiliated proxy terror groups of the regime in Iran. In the north, Israel has been bombarded with rockets from Hezbollah, another proxy terror group of the regime in Iran. These latter attacks created over 60,000 displaced Israelis from the northern border communities for which no international aid has been offered or given.[148] At the time of this writing, in the aftermath of October 7th, Israel's military is at war with Hamas in Gaza. The goals of the war include the return of all hostages, living and deceased, and the complete dismantling of Hamas's military and governing capacities in the Strip.[149]

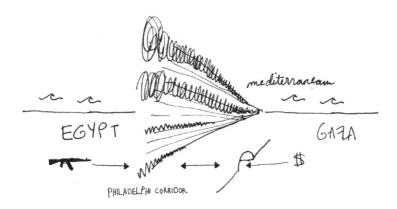

EGYPT

mediterranean

GAZA

PHILADELPHI CORRIDOR

Gaza's Border with Egypt

Until the October 7th massacre, due to a propaganda campaign that regularly characterized the Gaza Strip as an open-air prison, many were unaware that Gaza shares a border with Egypt called the **Philadelphi Corridor**. After the massacre, many questions arose, such as: *Why wouldn't Egypt, a fellow Arab nation, let in Palestinians to escape Israel's war with Hamas through this border?* The enormous fence that separates Egypt and Gaza boasts multiple layers of barbed wire and is magnitudes larger than the one placed along the Israel-Gaza border.[150] During Israel's military operation in the southern Gazan city of **Rafah** in 2024, the IDF found over one hundred tunnels between Gaza and Egypt, running right under the border wall itself.[151] Not only did these tunnels serve as a major method of resupplying arms to Hamas, but the taller and more ominous structure enabled Egyptian officials to better bribe travelers seeking passage.

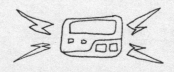

LEBANON, HEZBOLLAH, AND EXPLODING BEEPERS

On September 27th, 2024, a shipment of Taiwanese-manufactured pagers, ingeniously rigged with explosives, simultaneously detonated in the possession of key Hezbollah leaders. This attack, an unprecedented feat of military ingenuity on par with the legend of the Trojan Horse, disrupted Hezbollah's trust in their communications devices, forcing them to gather in person underground wherein the IDF targeted and eliminated much of Hezbollah's top leadership using bunker-buster bombs, including its chief, Hassan Nasrallah.[152] The world did a double take. Some argue that at this moment, Israel changed the narrative of the Oct 7th War from defense to offense. Why did this happen? On Oct 8th, 2023, only one day after the Oct 7th Massacre, Hezbollah, began an incessant rocket barrage in the north of Israel, displacing tens of thousands of Israelis and opened an immediate second front of the war. Some backstory: In 1978, after Lebanese-based Palestinian terrorists massacred thirty-eight Israeli civilians outside of Tel Aviv, Israel invaded Lebanon to push the terrorists away in what became known as the **First Lebanon War**. As a part of a brokered truce, the United Nations established **United Nations Interim Force in Lebanon (UNIFIL)**, to ensure stability of the Lebanese government after an Israeli withdrawal. Instead, UNIFIL allowed Hezbollah to build up weapons and infrastructure forcing Israel into the **Second Lebanon War** in 2006. With help from Iran, Hezbollah and UNIFIL turned southern Lebanon into a weapon against Israel. Since the exploding beeper incident, the IDF has uncovered networks of tunnels and weapons caches in close proximity to UNIFIL bases, yet another instance of UN corruption. The United States taxpayer has given $2.5 billion to UNIFIL since 2006 (see more on UN corruption in Chapter Six: The UN).[153]

THE DECLINE OF CHRISTIANITY IN THE MIDDLE EAST

The Jews are not the only ones whose populations have dramatically declined or been forced to relocate in the face of Islam. Over the last century many countries who had a sizable (and in the case of Lebanon, a majority) Christian population have dramatically decreased. Many Christians in this region are members of communities that predate Islam and can trace their roots back thousands of years. In 1930, Lebanon was 53% Christian, now it is 32%. In Syria the Christian population in 1930 was 14%, as of 2024 it's 1%.[155] Jordan's Christian population in 1930 was 20%, now it's 2%[156] Iraq's 1930 Christian population was 12% now it's .2%.[157] In Bethlehem, the population was roughly 80% Christian under Israeli control. However after the Palestinian Authority took over, the population has declined to roughly 10% Christian[158]. In Nazareth[159], the birthplace of Jesus, the population was majority Christian prior to 1948, however, now it's 70% Muslim and 30% Christian.[160]

WHERE ARE ALL THE JEWS IN THE MIDDLE EAST?

The answer is quite simple: they are mostly in Israel. Hundreds of thousands of Jews were expelled or otherwise forced out of their home countries in the Middle East between 1948 and 1979. None of these countries have ever made reparations to their Jewish communities or even acknowledged the persecution which took place. Jews commemorate the tragedy every November 30th (see Index: *Pogroms against Jews*).

Syria

Jews were placed under house arrest and forbidden from going to schools with Muslims. Bank accounts, property, and businesses were seized. Many were arrested and tortured. They were then forbidden from leaving Syria until late into the 20th century.

Iraq

Jews suffered pogroms and systematic discrimination at the hands of a Nazi-allied government. Many were arrested, tortured, and publicly executed. Thousands were robbed of their property, bank accounts, and other assets before being expelled and stripped of their citizenship.

Yemen

Jews faced centuries of antisemitic persecution at the hands of Yemenite Muslims. Centuries ago, Jews were required to give their first born son to a Muslim family. They were not allowed to speak in front of Muslims or to walk ahead of them. They were required to pay fees to Muslims to "protect" them. Later, they faced systemic legal discrimination and oppression and waves of barbaric violence. Tens of thousands of Yemenite Jews escaped Yemen in a daring **Mossad** (Israel's elite intelligence force) operation to liberate them from the appalling conditions they faced.

Algeria

Jews were robbed, beaten, arrested, murdered, and ultimately forced out of their homes. While Algeria was under Nazi occupation, Jews were stripped of their citizenship and their businesses were physically destroyed.

Egypt

One of the largest and most successful Jewish communities in the region was brutally oppressed with community leaders being targeted and arrested, accused of being "Zionist spies." Jews of Egypt lost their property, all assets, and any access to equal rights, and were put on ships with only one suitcase in hand. They were stripped of their citizenship and sent out of Egypt with no return or recourse for justice.

Tunisia

Jews of Tunisia were one of the only communities in the Arab World to be sent to concentration camps at the hands of the Nazis. Nazi antisemitism permeated parts of the Middle East, particularly North Africa. Jews in Tunisia faced similar dispossession of property and expulsions in addition to continued pogroms and violence against their communities.

THE FARHUD MASSACRE

On June 1-2,1941, the 2,900 year history of the thriving Jewish community in Baghdad, Iraq's capital, ended by way of an unprovoked massacre. The libel that Jews were benefiting from British colonialism spread amongst the Muslim community, which soon extended to classical antisemitic tropes of Jews controlling the economy and political parties. Iraqi media said: "The biggest enemies of mankind are those who believe the Jews." The Farhud was a massacre a long time in the making, though it still came as a shock. Hundreds of Jews were hanged, raped, and murdered in the streets of Baghdad, not unlike the October 7th Massacre of 2023 in southern Israel.[154]

A REGION IN FLUX

Repeated conflicts, foreign interventions, economic instability, and the presence of many religious communities puts the Middle East in a constant state of uncertainty. In addition to the Iranian Revolution, and the Lebanese, Yemeni, and Syrian Civil Wars, there has been near constant conflict in the region. In the 2010s, a series of protests against dictatorships in Egypt, Tunisia, and Syria known as the **Arab Spring** produced problems of which we are still facing the consequences, and even older wounds like America's 2003 War in Iraq have not healed.[161] One thing you can be certain of when learning more about the region is that very little as it stands today will be the reality tomorrow.

4

THE OCCUPATION

The word "occupation," often shouted through bullhorns by anti-Israel activists, carries a meaning and context often misunderstood. First, "**occupation**" is a legal term which describes territory won by a state through military action that is managed by that state until its status is decided in peace time.[162] Therefore, occupation is legal under international law. Many countries have occupied others in the past, including the United States, which after World War II, occupied Japan for seven years and Germany for forty-five years (the U.S. maintains 53,000 and 35,500 troops in Japan and Germany, respectively). The occupations of former enemies resulted in the building of some of America's strongest alliances: today, both Germany and Japan are thriving and peaceful democracies.[163]

Israel currently occupies the West Bank, which is the subject of this chapter. (Note, Israel did not occupy Gaza from 2005 until 2023, when they made a military incursion to protect themselves from the invading Hamas terrorists.) Beyond the legal distinction, the term "occupation" is often weaponized to denote a Jewish state existing in any borders whatsoever. In this chapter, we will discuss the "occupation" as it relates to Israel and the Palestinians, and examine the reality of what it means for Israelis and for the people living within occupied territory. We will start, of course, by going back in time.

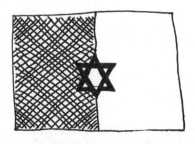

1924 ORIGINAL PALESTINE FLAG

CRITICAL EVENTS: OCCUPATION RELATED

As what remained of the once great Ottoman Empire was collapsing in the midst of the First World War, Britain and France, with the help of Russia, divided up the Middle Eastern territories in what is known as the **Sykes Piquot** agreement of 1916. In 1917, the British issued the **Balfour Declaration** which supported the establishment of a national homeland for the Jewish people in Palestine. In 1920, in the wake of the First World War, the newly minted **League of Nations** in San Remo, Italy, divided the lands of the recently defeated Ottoman Empire which included Syria, Iraq, and Palestine[164] (see maps *Ottoman Empire 1914 , French & British Mandates 1920*, and *1920 French & British MandateS: Lebanon, Syria, Palestine, Iraq*).

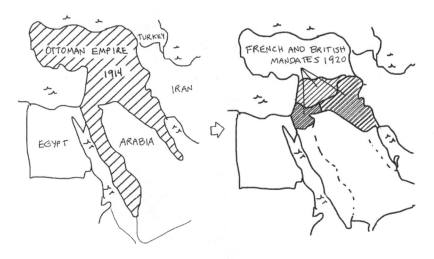

OTTOMAN EMPIRE 1914   FRENCH & BRITISH MANDATES 1920

Mandates were proposed to govern territories until a stable government was in place. The League of Nations understood that these territories would eventually "graduate" to full independent governance when the time was correct and the proper institutions were in place. Many territories in the Ottoman Empire became different types of mandates.

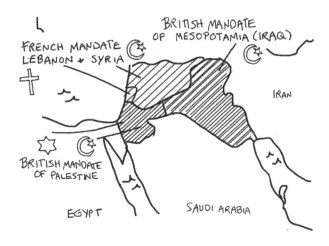

1920 FRENCH & BRITISH MANDATES: LEBANON, SYRIA, PALESTINE, IRAQ

The French Mandate was divided into two districts, Lebanon and Syria according to their majority populations of Christians and Muslims respectively. **The British Mandate for Palestine** was also further partitioned into two districts, with Palestine for the "National Homeland" of the Jewish People and **Transjordan**, now the Hashemite Kingdom of Jordan.

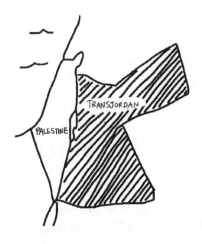

1921 ESTABLISHMENT OF TRANSJORDAN

After years of conflict verging on all out civil war between Arabs and Jews within British Palestine, and in the wake of the Second World War, on November 29, 1947, the United Nations voted to partition the Palestinian Mandate into a Jewish state and another Arab state (see map *1947 Partition Plan to Create a Jewish and Another Arab State*)[166].

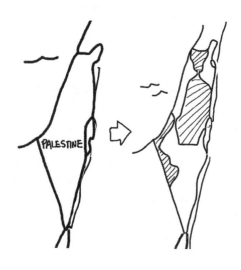

1947 PARTITION PLAN TO CREATE A JEWISH AND ANOTHER ARAB STATE

This division was based on a survey conducted by the UN, known as the **United Nations Special Committee on Palestine (UNSCOP)**. When UN representatives came to survey the populations, much of the Arab leadership boycotted the meetings, whereas the Jewish leadership met with the Committee members.[167] Despite the boycott of the meetings, the Arabs were offered the fertile farming lands, roughly half of the coastal plain, and the mountainous region critical for defense, while the Jews were offered the arid Negev desert and coastland that was infested with malaria. The United States and most democracies voted to approve the plan for partition. The Arab countries rejected it outright.

ISRAEL'S WAR OF INDEPENDENCE

On May 15, 1948, David Ben-Gurion declared the independence of the new state of Israel. Jordan, Syria, Egypt, Iraq, and Lebanon immediately declared and waged war on Israel, and Israel won after a year of bloody fighting, which had begun before the official declaration of the state. At the end of the Israeli War of Independence, Egypt occupied a piece of the southern coastal plain, soon to be called the Gaza Strip, and Jordan occupied a region to the direct west of the Jordan River, soon to be called the West Bank.

After the War of Independence, in 1949, Israel and its neighbors settled upon an **armistice line**, still today known as the **Green Line** because it was originally drawn with an imprecise green grease pencil two to three millimeters thick on a map. (See map below.)

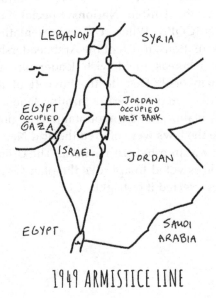

1949 ARMISTICE LINE

This line separated the new State of Israel from East Jerusalem and the West Bank which were controlled by the new nation of Jordan, and the Gaza Strip, occupied by Egypt. These were not official borders of the new state of Israel, but rather delineations to show where the Israeli military ended and where Arab militaries began.[168] (This same phenomenon can be seen in situations such as the "border" between North and South Korea, which is actually an armistice line.)

THE WAR OF 1967 / THE SIX DAY WAR

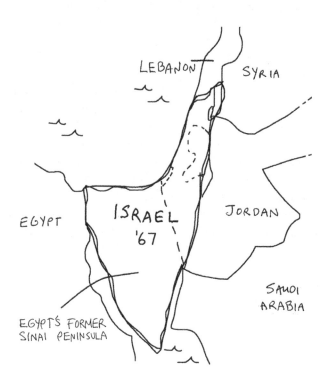

TERRITORIES GAINED IN THE SIX DAY WAR OF '67

The Six Day War *(cont.)*

In 1967, the Egyptian army closed off the Straits of Tiran in the Red Sea, a primary shipping port for Israel which constituted a legal act of war. Together with Syria, Jordan, and Iraq, Egypt began to amass armies on the Green Line. Launching a defensive preemptive strike, Israel defeated all invading Arab countries in six days, hence it is also referred to in Israel as **The Six Day War**. In the course of fighting, Israel's military blew past the Green Line, establishing Israeli control in East Jerusalem and the West Bank (from Jordan), the Gaza Strip and the Sinai Peninsula (from Egypt), and the Golan Heights (from Syria).[169] In six days, Israel had tripled its size (see map *Territories Gained in the Six Day War of '67*).

Months after the war, leaders from the Arab countries gathered in **Khartoum**, Sudan, and issued its three infamous no's: "**No negotiations, no recognition, and no peace with Israel**."[170] Israeli society was split over the issue of negotiating the status of the newly acquired territories. There were those who viewed them as a bargaining chip, to be offered in exchange for a permanent cease in hostilities. There were others who believed that because the territories had been acquired by Israel through defensive warfare, they were Israel's to keep.[171]

ירושלים

JERUSALEM UNITED

The Israeli securing of East Jerusalem during the 1967 War marks one the most dramatic moments in Jewish history. When Israeli troops marched through the iconic Roman-era gates in June 1967, the words of General Mordechai Gur, "The Temple Mount is in our hands!" electrified the nation.[172] After Israel's "capture," or "liberation," of East Jerusalem, religious liberty was restored to the holy sites, something that had always been denied under Jordanian occupation. Out of respect for Muslims, Israel offered the Jordanian religious authority control of the laws surrounding accession to the Temple Mount (Al-Aqsa compound). To this day, the Jordanian **Waqf** (an Islamic land endowment) supervises movement at the holiest site in Judaism.[173]

Because Israel officially annexed East Jerusalem, Palestinians residing there were offered citizenship and voting rights in compliance with international law. However, a vast majority of Palestinians opted not to accept citizenship, considering it would mean the "normalization of Israel."[174] Some critics say that the process of obtaining citizenship for Palestinians in East Jerusalem is not fair and should be made much easier.[175] This complicated situation has led to legal disputes over specific East Jerusalem properties like those in the neighborhood of **Sheikh Jarrah** and **Silwan**.[176] According to Israel and the United States, the status of East Jerusalem is not occupied, yet the on-the-ground reality of the city remains controversial.

WHO ARE THE PALESTINIAN PEOPLE?

In the years leading up to the Six Day War and especially following Israel's victory, the Arabs in The West Bank (occupied by Jordan) and Gaza (occupied by Egypt) began to increasingly identify themselves as "Palestinians."[177] Yet, the understanding of who is a "Palestinian" has shifted over time. There has never been a Palestinian state. The name itself is not mentioned once in the holy books of Judaism, Christianity, or Islam. The name Palestine, initially *"Syria Palestina"* was first given to the region when the Roman Emperor Hadrian elected to punish the Jews of the land who had revolted against Rome one too many times. As for the origin of the name, **Palestina** came from the word **Philistines**, an enemy nation of the Israelites, ethnic Greeks, from biblical times.[178]

Before 1948, during the British Mandate, it was the Jews of the land who had been mostly associated with the term "Palestinian." After Israel's establishment, the term "Palestinian" described mainly the refugee population from the War of Independence, and referred to both Arabs and Jews. But in the 1960s, an Egyptian named Yasser Arafat began to insist to Arab leaders that the "Palestinians" were a unique nation of their own, defined by exclusive Arab ancestry and by lost property in the land that was to become Israel from before 1948.

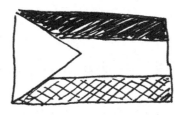

1964 PALESTINE FLAG

In 1964, Arafat founded the **Palestine Liberation Organization (PLO)**, a terrorist movement to wipe Israel off the map by any means necessary, and used the political party Fatah to organize and execute its mission.[179] The PLO's charter upheld that the Jewish people had no right to be in the land, let alone establish independence within it, and that it belonged to "Palestinians" alone, "from the river to the sea." Any place where there were Arab refugees displaced from the 1948 war became a defacto base for PLO terrorist activity as Arafat gained popularity. The PLO officially gained legitimacy from the Arab nations after the 1967 war when they could view the distinctive Palestinian people as pawns to move against Israel.[180] Israel's sudden control of huge Arab populations in the West Bank and Gaza gave credence to the idea of Israel as an oppressor, a very useful political weapon, especially in international bodies. Thus, the "Palestinians", as we understand them today, were born.

WHEN JEWS WERE PALESTINIANS

In the 1930s, the Jewish football (American soccer) team in "the land" which competed in international tournaments was called the **Palestine Football Team**. It had the logo of a Star of David on the jerseys, brandished blue and white colors, and was only renamed *Maccabi Tel Aviv* after 1948.[181] *The Jerusalem Post*, a popular newspaper in Israel today, was originally titled **The Palestine Post**, founded by a Zionist Jew in 1932.[182]

The Palestine Symphony Orchestra in the 1930s was a Jewish orchestra, later becoming the Israeli Philharmonic.[183] Palestine Airways was also founded by a Zionist Jew.[184] In 1948, when Arab nations united to attack and destroy the nascent modern state of Israel, the headline of the *Boston Globe* read, "Arabs Invade Palestine," referring to what was then known as a land called Palestine, filled with Palestinian Jews.[185]

1973 THE YOM KIPPUR WAR

The occupation gave a perfect cover for the Arab countries surrounding Israel to exploit the plight of the Palestinian people to their own populations to avoid them concentrating on the extreme societal inequities and failings of their own governments. Like the massacre of October 7th, 2023 which was launched on the Jewish holy day of Simchat Torah, in October of 1973, Egypt and Syria attacked Israeli forces on Yom Kippur in the Sinai Peninsula and the Golan Heights. It was a devastating surprise assault, which left over 2,500 IDF soldiers dead, but Israel ultimately prevailed with the help of a United States airlift of weapons and supplies.

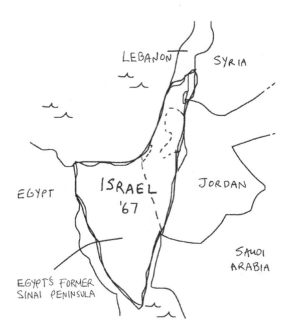

In 1977, Prime Minister Menachem Begin signed a peace deal with Egypt and traded the Sinai Peninsula for a cease in hostilities between the two countries. These negotiations led to the assassination of Egyptian President Anwar Sadat by radical Islamists.

GOLDA MEIR

One of Israel's most memorable Prime Ministers, **Golda Meir** led the country from 1969 to 1974. Meir famously insisted in a television interview that she and all Jews living in the land of Israel were Palestinian: "From 22 to 48, I carried a Palestinian passport. I am a Palestinian."[186] Born in Ukraine, Meir emigrated to the United States along with many other Jewish families fleeing antisemitic violence and persecution. Meir then moved to Mandatory Palestine in the 1920s and worked her way into the leadership of the growing Jewish community, eventually playing a major role in building the young state.[187] Meir made history as Israel's first female Prime Minister, beloved by many, yet was criticized for her handling of **The Yom Kippur War** in 1973 and "deciding not to decide," in regard to territories acquired after 1967.

SETTLEMENTS

Settlements are essentially clusters of homes that range from crude outposts to major cities with paved roads and shopping malls. The people who live in them are often referred to as **settlers**, (though many don't like the term.) After the 1967 war, many Israeli Jews within the religious Zionist sect saw Israel's newly acquired territory as not just a military victory, but a spiritual one. Prominent rabbis and their followers viewed the securing of the Old City of Jerusalem and the West Bank as a step toward fulfilling the commandment of settling the entire biblical land of Israel.[188] Though Israel formally annexed East Jerusalem in 1967 and offered full citizenship to the Arabs in the territory, it did not annex the West Bank in the process, rendering the Jews who moved into the territory as a kind-of legal anomaly: citizens of Israel subjected to Israeli law, while not residents of Israel.

Many of the people who moved to the West Bank after '67 did so to prevent an Israeli government from handing over control of the land and religious sites to another authority, like had been done with the Sinai Peninsula and Temple Mount. Today, many believe that the settlements in the West Bank provide a security buffer for larger Jewish areas within Israel. There are also people who move to the settlements for more practical reasons such as cheaper housing or a more pastoral life.[189] Settlements remain a divisive issue within Israel. Disputes over their legality shift depending upon differing U.S. administration's interpretation of international law, as do the attitudes about them within Israeli society itself.[190]

THE **S** WORD

LANGUAGE IS IMPORTANT:
"SETTLERS" AND "SETTLER VIOLENCE"

The term "settlers" is deployed in multiple ways that warrant clarifying. First, in a world where "decolonization" is brandished in every protest, antisemites/jihadists will often use the term "settler" as a pejorative term for *all* Israelis – including those who live in Tel Aviv and Jerusalem – to imply that Jews do not possess the right to self-determination anywhere in the land, and are a foreign, colonial presence. This has become a method of denying Israel's right to exist and perpetuating antisemitic tropes.[191]

Another term requiring clarification is **settler violence**. Because of the occupation, any presence of Jews in the West Bank creates flashpoints where Palestinians attack Israelis and Israelis attack Palestinians. One example of the former occurred in 2024 when a Palestinian terrorist opened fire on an Israeli civilian bus near the settlement of **Ariel**, wounding eight. The terrorist was neutralized by local IDF forces.[192] The latter type of violence, when Israelis commit violent offenses in the Occupied Territories is unacceptable and a direct challenge to Jewish values which prize the right to life and pursuit of peaceful co-existence above all else. Therefore, when someone within the settlement community initiates and/or commits any kind of violence, especially nationalist/religious-motivated violence, against Palestinians, as happened in 2024, when Israeli settlers rampaged through the cities of **Huwara** and **Jit**, vandalizing property, setting buildings and cars on fire, and terrorizing civilians,[193] this conduct is condemned by the majority of the Israeli population including the IDF and the security establishment.

However, while all violence of this manner is appalling, a new definition of "settler violence" has emerged in recent years in which the UN, eager to demonize Israel, conflates the definition to mean anything from Jews visiting the Temple Mount in Jerusalem to traffic accidents which occur in the West Bank. For example, between 2016 and 2022, The UN counted 5,656 documented incidents of *settler violence* against Palestinians. But criminology research revealed that 1,600 of these alleged incidents took place in Jerusalem, Israeli sovereign territory, with almost all of them involving Jews entering the Temple Mount, or described clashes between the Israeli police and worshippers who acted violently in the area.[194]

1987 THE FIRST INTIFADA

In the late 1980s, as the occupation of the West Bank and Gaza entered its third decade, Palestinians launched an uprising named "the intifada" in Arabic, literally meaning "shaking off,"which at first began as riots and protests in response to a traffic incident between an Israeli and a group of Palestinians, but rapidly accelerated into direct attacks against the IDF and acts of terror against Israelis both in the West Bank and in Israeli sovereign territory.[195] During this time, Palestinians spread lies that Israel was indiscriminately murdering Palestinians, which led to increased violence, including Molotov cocktail and stone-throwing attacks against the IDF and civilians alike, leaving more than 1,400 Israeli civilians and 1,700 Israeli soldiers wounded. Jews were not the only victims of the violence.

In fact, the number of Arabs killed for political and other reasons by Palestinian death squads exceeded the number killed in clashes with Israeli troops. PLO Chairman Yasser Arafat defended the killing of Arabs deemed to be "collaborating with Israel."[196] At the end of the bloodshed, Israeli society seemed determined to explore political avenues that would bring peace, rather than more violence. Because this burst of terrorism and violence by Palestinians against Israeli civilians happened again a few decades later, this time period is known as The First Intifada.

1993 OSLO ACCORDS

In the early 1990s, after the strife of the First Intifada, the **Oslo Accords**, or, the Oslo Peace Process, began with secret meetings between Israel, the United States, and the PLO in Oslo, Norway. [197] In 1993, Israel agreed to recognize Palestinian political independence in the occupied territories of the West Bank and Gaza via a legitimized, new version of the PLO called the **Palestinian Authority (PA)**, with Arafat serving as the de facto leader of this new body and Israel's chief negotiating partner.[198] For their effort, Arafat, US President Bill Clinton, Israel's Defense Minister Shimon Peres, and Prime Minister Yitzhak Rabin received the Nobel Peace Prize. The Accords mandated that the PA would be a *temporary* governing body for Palestinians in the West Bank and Gaza as negotiations continued, meaning that construction of Israeli settlements would end. The PA was meant to become "null and void" once an independent Palestinian state was established.

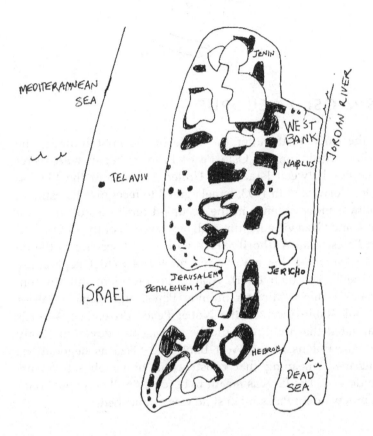

MEDITERANNEAN SEA

JENIN

JORDAN RIVER

WEST BANK

NABLUS

TEL AVIV

JERICHO

ISRAEL

JERUSALEM
BETHLEHEM †

HEBRON

DEAD SEA

AREAS ☐ = A ■ = B Everything Else = C THE WEST BANK

You must be wondering, why so crazy?

AREAS A, B, AND C – WHY SO CRAZY?

The Oslo Accords divided the West Bank into three zones: Areas A, B, and C. These "areas" were intended to be a temporary status agreement, predicated on both sides reaching a long term solution. The framework of Oslo still stands in the West Bank, dividing the territory according to population and security concerns. Areas A, B, and C are essential to understanding the nature of Israel's relationship with the Palestinians.

AREA A

Area A is home to about 90% of Palestinians in the West Bank and was designated during Oslo to be administered completely by the Palestinian Authority.[200] This means that both civil and security control in the area are the obligation of Palestinian leadership. Area A includes Nablus, Jenin, and Ramallah, and is strictly forbidden territory for Israeli civilians to enter. In the past several years, Nablus and Jenin have become hotbeds of terrorist activity against Israelis, which has led the Israeli military to carry out operations within Area A to protect its civilians.

AREA B

Area B, which includes the outskirts of Palestinian cities in Area A and areas near the Green Line, was designated during Oslo negotiations to be under **joint Israeli-Palestinian** control. The Palestinian Authority is meant to oversee civil affairs, while Israel manages security. This means that the IDF is allowed to conduct operations within the zone to prevent terrorism, but issues of land jurisdiction, construction, education, healthcare, and transportation are the prerogatives of the Palestinian Authority.[202] Some radical Israeli settlers have been accused of undermining the Palestinian Authority's jurisdiction over its citizens by themselves policing agricultural fields and protesting against Palestinian construction of buildings, behavior which has led to violent and deadly riots.[203]

ISRAELI CITIZENS NOT ALLOWED

Area A is extremely dangerous for Israeli Jews to enter and signs put up by the Israeli government forbid them to do so. During the Second Intifada, two Israeli civilians, **Vadim Nurzhitz** and **Yosef "Yossi" Avrahami**, mistakenly entered the city of Ramallah in Area A. Both Nurzhitz and Avrahami were brutally tortured and then murdered by Palestinians living in the area. In a now famous picture from the incident, a man inside the building where Nurzhitz and Avrahami were being held captive shows his bloodstained hands to a crowd of cheering rioters outside, joyfully telling them that the Israelis had been killed.[201]

AREA C
Area C, though entirely in the West Bank, is under Israeli civil and military control. The vast majority of Israeli settlements are in Area C of the West Bank, though Palestinians also live in the zone. The presence of Palestinians who do not have Israeli citizenship versus Jews who do have Israeli citizenship in the area produces a maze of legal complications and security considerations. Local disputes are often brought before the Israeli Supreme Court.[204]

HEBRON AND THE TOMB OF THE PATRIARCHS AND MATRIARCHS

The only Israeli settlement to exist *within* a Palestinian community is the Jewish village of **Kiryat Arba** next to the ancient city of Hebron. Hebron is home to the Caves of the Patriarchs, which Jews and also Muslims in the West Bank believe to be the burial place of Abraham, Isaac, Jacob, Rachel, Leah, and Sarah. The Palestinian Authority and Israel negotiated the status of Hebron outside of the Oslo Accords, in the **Hebron Protocol**, establishing a permanent Israeli military presence to protect the ancient Jewish community within the territory.[205] However, sometimes the religious and political leanings of the residents of Hebron and the adjacent settlement of Kiryat Arba clash with the surrounding Palestinian population who are sympathetic to Hamas which makes the city a hotbed for national disputes and occasional violence.

In 1994, a man by the name of **Baruch Goldstein** claimed that he had heard Palestinians in the Ibrahimi Mosque (the Muslim section of the Tomb of the Patriarchs) plotting violence against the Jewish community of Hebron. Goldstein entered the **Ibrahimi Mosque** and killed twenty-nine Palestinian worshippers over the Jewish holiday of Purim.[206] The terrible massacre was widely condemned in Israeli society and around the world, most forcefully by then-Prime Minister Yitzhak Rabin.

YITZHAK RABIN

In 1995, at the height of negotiations between Israelis, Americans, and Palestinians, Prime Minister Yitzhak Rabin was assassinated in Tel Aviv by far-right Israeli law student Yigal Amir.[199] Though tragic, his assassination did not derail the peace process between Israel and the Palestinians, as we will discuss later. Yitzhak Rabin was born in Jerusalem and dedicated his early life to the pre-Israel Jewish community's defense, eventually becoming Chief of Operations for the **Palmach**, an elite fighting unit during the 1948 War of Independence. Rabin served as the IDF's Chief of Staff in the 1967 War, Ambassador to the United States from 1968 to 1973, and Israel's Minister of Defense during the 1980s. In 1992, Rabin was elected Prime Minister on a platform of supporting the peace process between Israelis and Palestinians, and in 1994, he won the Nobel Peace Prize for his role in the Oslo Accords.

2000 CAMP DAVID STATEHOOD OFFER

In August 2000 at Camp David, an American Presidential Retreat in Maryland, then Israeli Prime Minister Ehud Barak offered Yasser Arafat a Palestinian state: 98% of the West Bank with land swaps out of Israel, all of the Gaza Strip, and a capital in East Jerusalem. It was a monumental offer that thrilled the Americans and a large part of the international community. Yet, instead of accepting the offer, Arafat descended from his private plane into the West Bank and declared that Barak's terms were not acceptable.[207] Many attribute Arafat's "no" at Camp David to the realization that had he signed, the Palestinians would no longer receive international legitimacy and aid for their violence against Israelis, and their fight of "from the river to the sea," i.e., eliminating Israel as a Jewish state, would really be over.

2000 THE SECOND INTIFADA

The negotiations formally ended during the outbreak of the Second Intifada, a bloody campaign of bombings and shooting against Israeli civilians (instigated by Arafat): the **Dolphinarium Massacre** in Tel Aviv, leaving more than 20 mostly young people dead; the Sbarro Pizza bombing in Jerusalem, killing families and tourists; and the **Netanya Seder Massacre** at a hotel, which killed dozens of people, including Holocaust survivors, during the annual celebration of Passover.[208] Before the October 7th Massacre of 2023, many remember the Second Intifada as the darkest time to live in Israel.

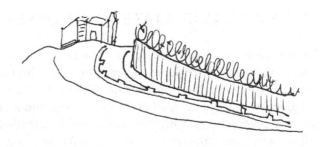

The Security Barrier

The Second Intifada shattered Israeli's sense of safety. In order to quell the wave of terror, the IDF enhanced security in the West Bank, deploying many measures that are in place to this day. This includes the **security barrier**, often referred to as the "wall" or "fence," which is a physical barrier built by Israel in the West Bank with the intention of preventing terrorist attacks. It has been enormously effective, but the Palestinians with work permits who commute to Israel don't like the delays it causes.[209] The Palestinian Authority often claims that the wall was constructed in order to oppress their population and to cut off Palestinians communities, but in reality, the wall was constructed as a temporary measure in direct response to the uptick in sniper attacks and suicide bombers during the Second Intifada.[210] Less than 5% of the entire security barrier is constructed with concrete.[211] The majority is a small wire and in some cases no fence at all, simply a sensor that alerts security when someone has illegally crossed.[212]

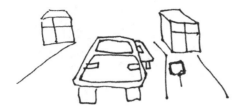

Checkpoints

Checkpoints, constructed after the Second Intifada, are found throughout the West Bank usually at the entrance to sovereign Israeli territory or to settlements. Checkpoints are designed to further protect Israeli citizens by way of monitoring movement of weapons and dangerous individuals throughout the West Bank.[213] The checkpoints allow tens of thousands of Palestinians to pass into Israel every day, where many receive higher salaries and better benefits for their labor than they would under the Palestinian Authority.[214] Checkpoints remain controversial because of their effect on Palestinian freedom of movement within the West Bank.

GAZA

2005 ISRAELI TOTAL GAZA WITHDRAWAL

Up until this point, we have been discussing The West Bank. Now let us turn southward to the tiny piece of land on the Mediterranean Sea known as the Gaza Strip, which was occupied by Egypt until the Six Day War of '67. The legal Israeli occupation of Gaza ended when Prime Minister **Ariel Sharon** made the controversial decision in 2005 to remove the entirety of Israel's army from the Strip along with thousands of Jewish Israelis from their homes in the settlement of Gush Khatif inside the Gaza Strip.[215] International pressure and the rapidly increasing population of Palestinians in the area led Israel's centrist government and a majority of Israeli society to agree with the move. The move was widely seen as a step toward a two-state solution, if the Palestinians in Gaza were indeed willing to lay down their weapons and build a better life for themselves.

THE RISE OF HAMAS

Unfortunately, the exact opposite happened. Shortly after Israel's disengagement from Gaza, a Palestinian civil war ensued between Fatah and another political party, far more religious, violent, and radical than Fatah: Hamas. Hamas began brutally executing Fatah supporters and a Palestinian civil war ensued, shocking the entire world.[216] Hamas eventually staged a phony election and used violent coercion to solidify their power. There hasn't been an election held in Gaza since. The rivalry between Hamas and Fatah remains an important fault line in Palestinian politics today. Since Fatah's defeat in Gaza, Hamas and other terrorist groups have arisen in the West Bank to challenge its power, meaning the legitimacy of the Palestinian Authority, including Palestinian Islamic Jihad (PIJ) and **Lion's Den**.[217]

The Blockade
The Palestinian Civil War was followed by an outburst of attacks on Israel from Hamas which led to Israel establishing a *blockade* over the Gaza Strip, supervising the movement of goods and travel in and out of the Hamas-controlled enclave.[218] Note that a "blockade" is not "occupation," and any nation with a terrorist army on its borders would take the same actions as Israel".[219] Israel did not occupy Gaza from 2005 to 2023. After the Oct 7th War, the IDF has entered Gaza and at the time of this writing is dismantling Hamas' terror infrastructure.

HAMAS' ABUSE STRATEGIES

Human Shields
Hamas surrounds themselves with civilians and civilian infrastructure when engaged in warfare against Israel.[223] Homes, hospitals, and schools store weapons and terrorists and lie atop tunnels, making them legitimate military targets according to international law.[224] When Israel notifies Gazans to leave conflict areas or evacuate buildings before airstrikes, Hamas tells Gazans to do the opposite: to shelter in place to prevent Israel from carrying out strikes. This only leads to more civilian casualties.[225]

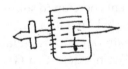

Journalism as a Weapon
There is no freedom of speech in Gaza, and therefore, international correspondents regularly report threats and censorship for reporting the truth about Hamas.[226] Some of the local journalists in Gaza are active members of Hamas themselves.[227] Numerous "photojournalists" in Gaza followed Hamas into Israel during the October 7th Massacre, calling into question the role of journalism in conflict zones.[228] Since Hamas raises money when images of wounded or dead Palestinians are broadcast and reported, "journalists" regularly inflate casualty numbers and stage elaborate productions of fake massacres supposedly committed by Israel, known in the media as **Pallywood**.[229]

THE ORIGINS OF HAMAS

The origins of Hamas are striking. In 1973, an Islamic cleric living in Gaza named **Sheikh Ahmed Yassin** founded the Palestinian Branch of the Muslim Brotherhood. In 1987, this same Sheikh founded its Paramilitary Branch, which he called Hamas, with the help of **Sheikh Abdallah Azzam**. Azzam, as it so happens, was also the mentor of Osama Bin Laden and helped him start Al Qaeda, the same terrorist network responsible for 9/11.[220] The original **Hamas Charter** called for the destruction of Israel (Article 13) and the genocide of Jews living there (Article 7).[221] The Hamas charter does not, contrary to popular belief, seek Palestinian liberation in an independent state. Hamas, in Arabic, stands for "Islamic Resistance Movement," a nod to the organization's use of **jihad** to achieve their political goals. "Jihad," originally described in the Qu'ran as a spiritual struggle to turn one into a better Muslim, also refers to the Islamic militia tactic of slaughtering innocent people in the name of satisfying God, otherwise known as fundamentalist terrorism.[222] October 7th is a prime example of Hamas's use of jihad, a practice shockingly funded by the Qatari regime and the Islamic Republic of Iran.

ISRAEL'S EFFORTS TO ASSIST THE PALESTINIANS: COGAT

After the Oslo Accords, Israel created the **Coordinator of Government Activities in the Territories, COGAT**, which is responsible for coordinating civilian issues between Israel and the Palestinian territories in the West Bank.[230] COGAT also oversees the transfer of humanitarian aid to Gaza during wartime, the granting of construction permits to Palestinians, facilitating medical assistance to Palestinians in need, and other humanitarian programs. COGAT is also responsible for the demolition of illegal construction in the West Bank, both Jewish and Palestinian, though whether or not there is a bias against Palestinian construction remains a point of controversy.[231] During the recent 2023 Israel-Hamas war, COGAT established a Gaza division to oversee the transfer of humanitarian aid into the enclave.

The Palestinian and Hamas' Abuse of Permits

One of the biggest challenges for COGAT is that the permits granted to Palestinians – including emergency medical permits for patients to receive specific treatments in Israel for terminal diseases like cancer – are often abused by terrorist organizations to threaten and blackmail innocent Palestinians. There have been repeated incidents of medical patients being forced to transfer goods or cash to Palestinian terrorists from the West Bank when they were permitted to enter Israel. [232]

The Israeli-Palestinian Joint Water Committee

The Israeli-Palestinian Joint Water Committee, JWC, was established in 1995 as a part of the Oslo Accords to coordinate water usage and sewage between Israel and the Palestinians. Today, Israel provides beyond what the Oslo Accords stipulate, but Palestinian leaders often sabotage water access in order to plead for more international funding. Here are several examples:

1. Palestinian officials frequently refuse to update Palestinian population statistics so they can claim Israel is restricting water usage later.[233]
2. Palestinian officials falsely accuse Israel of limiting water to Palestinians but providing it to nearby settlers. This is false, because the water pipes (as well as electricity grids) are not divided by nationality. Israel also desalinates seawater and treats wastewater, and pumps this back into the joint aquifer for the use of both populations, in addition to stabilizing the aquifer for future generations.[234]
3. Palestinians also have illegally drilled into pipes throughout the West Bank to obtain water, meaning those who receive water further away will not have enough.[235]
4. When Hamas entirely ruled Gaza, Palestinians falsely accused Israel of restricting water but their crisis was as a result of an aging sewage and water filtration system which the Palestinian Authority refused to repair or fund due to their political grievances with Hamas.[236] Hamas also refused to fund such renovations and diverted their funds to terrorism. Hamas also unearthed existing pipes to create rockets to shoot at Israel.

THE APARTHEID LIE

The false accusation of **apartheid** against Israel is a libel to turn people against the Jewish state. An apartheid system is defined by a government that gives different services to people within a country according to race. For example, from 1948 to 1994 in Apartheid South Africa, black and white people were completely segregated. Black South Africans were forbidden to work with whites and were barred from fields such as politics, medicine, law, entertainment, and more. Separation even occurred in daily life, with designated bus stops, water fountains, and beaches for different races.[238] The system of governance in the West Bank – to which Israel and the Palestinian Authority agreed in the Oslo Accords – stipulates that Israel's laws apply to the 60 percent of the territory which Israel governs and where Israelis reside, and the PA applies its laws to the 40 percent that it governs, where 98 percent of the Palestinian Arabs live.[239] That's not apartheid; that's an agreed-upon division of rights and responsibilities.

Israel's laws in these territories are not based on race, which is the essence of apartheid; they are based on citizenship, just like a Mexican citizen wouldn't have the same rights and laws as an American citizen if he was visiting San Diego from Tijuana. The Palestinian Arab residents of the territories are not Israeli citizens, so they vote in the Palestinian Authority's elections when the PA allows them. The Palestinian Authority hasn't held an election since 2006 for fear of not winning and is effectively an authoritarian regime under Mahmood Abbas. [240]

In Israel's sovereign territory laws apply equally to Israeli citizens of all colors: White, Black, and in between; Jew, Christian, and Muslim. Arabs and Jews work, study, and live side-by-side and are entitled to the same political rights. Arab citizens of Israel constitute 30% of the country's doctors, despite being only 20% of the population, are an estimated 50% of the pharmacists, and a fair proportion of the police force.[241] Some even serve in the IDF. Discrimination in employment is illegal, as is segregation in any public space. All Israeli citizens are eligible to vote in Israeli elections.[242]

ELECTRICITY

Electricity is also the subject of disputes in the West Bank and in Gaza. In Gaza, in particular, power shortages occur frequently. The PA is responsible for paying Gaza's electricity bills and they pay Israel's electric company for providing it. But due to the political rivalry, Fatah has no interest in Hamas being successful and refuses to pay for Gaza's electricity.[237] Israel is not permitted to negotiate directly with Hamas, as the PA is the official Palestinian leadership. The people of Gaza suffer at the hands of their own leaders because of it. Israel often gets blamed regardless.

A Case for Settlements

Many who support the settlement project in the West Bank believe that building Jewish homes on land won in the Six Day War improves Israel's security by providing a barrier between terrorism and Israeli population centers like Jerusalem and Tel Aviv. These supporters believe that removing Jewish civilians with Israeli citizenship from occupied territory endangers the security of Israelis by creating a vacuum. Some argue that this was proven true after the Jews left Gaza in 2005 which resulted in a de facto terror state leading to the October 7th Massacre of 2023. Some religious sects also believe that settling historically Jewish land, including holy cities like Hebron, Jericho, and Nablus, will hasten the coming of the Jewish Messiah, which will in turn redeem the Jewish people and bring peace to all the world. There are also segments of both religious and secular communities who support settlements on the basis of the argument that Jews should be able to live in their indigenous homeland, regardless of political considerations. Some Jews interpret international law to mean that disputed territories in the West Bank and Gaza are not "occupied," because they were never part of a sovereign nation (there has never been an independent state of Palestine). Others feel that the Palestinians' multiple missed opportunities to create a peaceful state next to Israel over the last seventy five plus years justify annexing territory via settlements for security.[243]

A Case Against Settlements

Those against settlements also have many reasons, including the **Fourth Geneva Convention**, which states that the act of moving citizens into occupied territory and awarding them citizenship rights under the occupying power while denying those same rights to others based on nationality constitutes a denial of equality under the law, a core principle of democracy.[244] Others argue that settlements jeopardize the longevity of Israel by de facto incorporating millions of Arab Muslims into the apparatus of the state and threatening Israel's clear Jewish majority. Additionally, many claim that settlements harm Israel's security capabilities by expanding the length of its borders and the soldiers necessary to protect Jewish communities. Indeed, before the October 7th Massacre of 2023, the number of soldiers in the West Bank was more than those stationed at the Jordanian, Syrian, Lebanese, Egyptian, and Gaza border – combined.[245] Opponents to settlements are also against the restrictions to Palestinians' movement in the West Bank that they have cause, citing human and political rights that all democracies should prioritize. It is important to note that many Israelis also support settlement blocs such as **Gush Etzion**, a West Bank settlement that was abandoned during the 1948 war, as these are territories that will be included in any future peace agreement, but oppose the expansion of settlements.

OBSTACLES FOR PEACE

Like any other country, Israel's first obligation is to protect its own people. Today, Palestinian society is fractured by sectarian violence and terrorist organizations that are funded and supported by the Islamic Republic of Iran, Qatar, and even the United States under the guise of humanitarian aid (more on this later). Many believe Israel doesn't have the luxury of unilateral withdrawal from the West Bank because it would render too many Israeli cities indefensible from Palestinian terrorists, considering the elevation of the West Bank (cities like Tel Aviv are at sea level.) On the Israeli side, extremists who commit settler violence undermine Israel's peace efforts. The greatest obstacle of all, however, is whether or not Israel has a legitimate partner in the first place. Israel has extended its hand countless times and at great expense. But thus far, Palestinian leaders have proven more committed to the concept of "from the river to the sea" (a.k.a. wiping Israel off the map) than they are to ensuring a brighter future for their people.

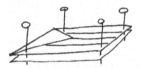

PALESTINIAN STATEHOOD REJECTIONISM

1937 The Peel Commission, a European envoy of researchers, recommends 80% of the land between the river and the sea to an independent Palestinian Arab state. The Arab nations reject it.[246]

1947 The UN Partition Plan divides 55% of the land to an independent Arab state and 45% to a Jewish state. The Arab states reject it.[247]

1967 UN Resolution 242 produces the "land for peace" equation for lasting calm in the Middle East. The PLO rejects it.[248]

1995 The Oslo Accords described above are originally accepted by the PLO, now the PA, but deteriorate when Araftat refuses to stop terror.

2000 Camp David Summit, Prime Minister Ehud Barak offers 97% of the West Bank and the entirety of the Gaza Strip to the Palestinians. Arafat rejects it.

2008 Secret Offer - Prime Minister **Ehud Olmert** offers 98% of the West Bank to the Palestinians, with land swaps out of Israel to compensate for the settlements. Mahmoud Abbas rejects it, due to no "right of return" of Palestinian "refugees" within the proposal.[249]

2019 The Trump Administration presents a plan for Palestinian state in the West Bank with land swaps out of Israel.[250] The Palestinians refuse to attend negotiations.

RECAP: THE OCCUPATION IN 60 SECONDS

1947-48 The State of Israel is Born

The United Nations votes to further partition the former British Mandate of Palestine, giving Arabs the fertile farming lands, roughly half the coastal plain, and the mountainous region to the east, critical for defense. The Jews are given the arid Negev desert and the parts of the coastland that were infested with malaria. The Arab countries reject the proposal outright. Jordan, Syria, Egypt, Iraq and Lebanon immediately declare war on Israel and lose. Egypt occupies the Gaza Strip and Jordan occupies the West Bank. Israel wins and declares her independence.

1964 PLO is Formed

After years of terror attacks and trouble on Israel's borders, in 1964, the Egyptian-born son of a man from Gaza named Yasser Arafat creates the concept of the Palestinian people (that excludes Jews) and the Palestinian Liberation Organization (PLO), a militia dedicated to Israel's destruction.

1967 Six Day War

Arab armies launch, and lose, another war against Israel which ends with Israel tripling its size: occupying the West Bank, the Gaza Strip, the Golan Heights, East Jerusalem, and the Sinai Peninsula.

1970s The PLO Wreaks Havoc

In 1971, the PLO, led by Arafat and based in Jordan, attempted to overthrow Jordanian **King Hussein**. 25,000 Palestinians die and tens of thousands are expelled from the country in the Jordanian Civil War also known as **Black September**. In 1972, Palestinian terrorists, under the banner of Black September, murder 12 Israeli Olympians at the Munich Olympics known as The Munich Massacre. In 1976, the PLO moved to overthrow the Lebanese government, drawing Israel into the First Lebanon War. Over 100,000 civilians are killed and millions of refugees are created in the **Lebanese Civil War.** In 1979, Arafat and PLO lent their support to the overthrow of the Shah of Iran and the new Islamic Republic in Iran.

1973 The Yom Kippur War

Egypt and Syria attack Israel's forces in the Sinai and the Golan Heights in what is known as the Yom Kippur War and then lose.

1979 - 1981 Giving and Getting Land for Peace and Deterrence

In 1979, Israel gave the entire Sinai Peninsula it had acquired in 1967 back to Egypt in exchange for peace. In 1981, Israel annexes the Golan Heights to deter further attacks from Syria and Lebanon against Israeli civilians.

1982 Formation of Hezbollah in Lebanon

Palestinian collaboration with Hezbollah, an Iranian proxy terrorist organization, begins.

1987 The First Intifada Begins

Palestinians launch an uprising against Israel in the West Bank and Gaza that spills into Israel proper.

RECAP: THE OCCUPATION IN 60 SECONDS (CONT.)

1993 Oslo Accords Brokers Temporary Peace with Arafat and Legitimizes the PLO
After years of bloodshed, Israeli society seeks political avenues that would bring peace, rather than more violence. A deal is struck with Arafat/PLO to become the Palestinian Authority and share control over the occupied territories of the West Bank and Gaza.

2000 Palestinians Reject State Offer and Second Intifada Begins
Ehud Barak offers a state to the Palestinians including 97% of the West Bank and the Gaza Strip at Camp David. Arafat rejects the offer, and the Second Intifada begins, a campaign of bloody terrorism against Israeli civilians.

2005 Israel Withdraws from Gaza Entirely
Israel pulls out all troops and civilians out of the Gaza Strip without negotiating with the Palestinians first. From 2005 until 2023, Israel does not occupy the Gaza Strip. Hamas, a violent terrorist organization dedicated to Israel's destruction, seizes power.

2008 Palestinian Authority Rejects Statehood Again
Prime Minister Ehud Olmert offers an even better deal than in 2000: 98% of the West Bank. Mahmoud Abbas, President of the Palestinian Authority, rejects the offer.

2019 Palestinians Ignores Trump Peace Plan to Rebuild, Invest and Land Swap
The Trump Administration presents a plan for a Palestinian state in the West Bank with land swaps out of Israel. The Palestinians refuse to attend negotiations.

2020 Abraham Accords

UAE, Bahrain, and Sudan, soon followed by Morocco, recognize Israel in an economic normalization agreement

2023 October 7th Massacre

Hamas in the Gaza Strip launches the most brutal massacre in Israeli history. Israel responds.

POSSIBILITIES AFTER THE OCCUPATION

One State

A "one state solution" would mean that Israel absorbs all of the Palestinians in its midst with equal rights for all which would eventually end Jewish characteristics of the state due to the higher birth rates of Muslims within the territory over time. This means that Jewish aspects of the country, including the flag embroidered with the Star of David, the anthem *Hatikvah*, and the **Law of Return**, which automatically grants Israeli citizenship to every Jew in the world, would invariably cease. Israel would also likely lose its democracy, mirroring its numerous neighboring Arab countries. Jews would ultimately lose their right of self-determination and the protection Israel offers Jews around the world.

One State with Regional Rights

One state with "regional rights," meaning Israelis and Palestinians "coexist," in theory, but Palestinians in the West Bank and Gaza would only have regional, not political, rights, like the opportunity to vote for representatives in the Knesset. This undemocratic solution would require discriminatory laws on the basis of race, some would say akin to apartheid. Others would argue that Arabs who stay in Israel would enjoy the freedoms and per capita prosperity that Israel offers but not be able to vote in elections similar to the United States' relationship with Puerto Rico where citizens enjoy regional rights, live in a U.S. Territory but cannot vote in American elections.[251] Regardless of the framing, such a solution would likely unleash world condemnation but would preserve a Jewish state in symbols and laws, but not in population.

Two State Solution

This oft-repeated goal envisions Israeli and Palestinian states living side by side with self-determination for both peoples in the land, preserving Israel as a democracy and a Jewish-majority nation. This could only work if the neighboring Palestinian state declined to become a terrorist nation whose primary goal is to destroy Israel. Further, this new Arab state would have to reckon with their refusal to allow Jews to live in their state when millions of Arabs live in Israel. In the wake of the October 7th Massacre of 2023 originating from Hamas in Gaza, and the continued support of it within the West Bank, this dream seems far from reality unless there is a fundamental change in Palestinian society. Some who support a two-state solution support a confederation plan, in which Israelis living east of the Green Line are allowed to live in the state of Palestine as Israeli citizens, provided Israel allows as many Palestinians to live in Israel as citizens of Palestine, with freedom of movement between countries.[252]

Jordan as Palestine

Some propose, based on the original partitioning of British Palestine in 1922, that Jordan, which already has an approximately 65% Palestinian population, should serve as the Palestinian state. In 1922, the British installed the Hashemite family of Saudi Arabia, known for their rule over the city of Mecca, as rulers of the new country. In 1946, the Hashemites declared independence from Britain, as Israel would do two years later. In this scenario, cities that have large Palestinian populations within the Palestinian territories such as the West Bank would be demilitarized and attached to neighboring Jordan – which might consider calling itself "Palestine" to reflect the population.[253]

The "No Solution," or, a Final Border

Israel draws a final border near the Green Line, deciding officially which settlements are within Israel and which are not, and remains agnostic on what happens to the Palestinians on the other side of the border. Whether they work towards a state of their own, or in collaboration with a coalition designed for this purpose, or are absorbed into the wider Arab world, or continue to hurt themselves with internal violence, Israel's main obligation will be to guard its final border and to guard it well.

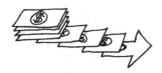

FOLLOW THE MONEY

Military occupations can last a few years, or they can last for several decades and end when an agreement is made to grant occupied people sovereignty, the act of self-governance. Why, you may ask, has the Israeli occupation lasted so long? Because, as discussed above, Palestinian leadership has rejected the establishment of a state of their own multiple times since 1967. Why would people who profess to want freedom and self governance always say no? The answer is money and power, which we will discuss in detail in the next chapter.

5

THE STICK UP

When people profit from selling something, it is known as a business, and in the case of the Israeli-Palestinian conflict, the product being sold is Palestinian suffering, and the customer is the international community. For the last seventy-six years, a handful of organizations and individuals have enriched themselves with money and power at the expense of a better future for the people on the ground they often claim to be representing. In this chapter, we will take a closer look at this business model and how it works. The first place to see the corruption at play in the Israeli-Palestinian conflict is within the subject of refugees. First, a bit of history:

THE CENTURY OF THE REFUGEE

The twentieth century, also known as "the century of the refugee," saw nearly 100 million displaced people from multiple world wars, regional wars, and civil wars.[254] The India-Pakistan partition after World War II led to 15 million refugees alone. This situation was managed largely by the **United Nations High Commission for Refugees, UNHCR**, an organization established in 1950 to face the enormous challenge of population movement. The UNHCR re-established millions of people in Hungary, Yugoslavia, Rwanda, Hong Kong, Vietnam, and Cambodia. Another successful organization, the United Nations Korean Reconstruction Agency, **UNKRA**, resettled 3.1 million Koreans in a span of three years after the outbreak of the Korean War in 1952. During this time, all but one of the populations which moved across borders were permanently resettled.

Who is a Refugee?

The United Nations defines a refugee as someone who has been forced to flee his or her country because of persecution, war, or violence.[255] According to the 1951 United Nations Refugee Convention and its 1967 protocols, an individual ceases to be a refugee upon their becoming a citizen of a new nation and establishing themselves under this nation's protection, and/ or being settled in a "third country" – a country following the initial country in which the refugee sought protection. **All refugees, with the exception of Palestinians, around the world are resettled by the UNHCR.**

UNRWA and the Perpetual Palestinian Refugee

Shortly after Israel's 1948 War of Independence, a *temporary* United Nations agency was created: **United Nations Reliefs and Works Agency** aka **UNRWA**, to provide immediate relief for those displaced in Israel's War of Independence. UNRWA was widely assumed to be merged into the UNHCR in the early '50s, and become another refugee success story. In 1950, **King Abdullah of Jordan** expressed his full intention to naturalize the Arab refugees residing in his borders, committing to awarding them Jordanian citizenship. But the other Arab leaders did not want to merge UNRWA with the UNHCR. They did not want to resettle the Palestinian Arab refugees from the war of 1948 and end their refugee status. Envoys to the United Nations from Egypt, Lebanon, and Saudi Arabia demanded that the UNHCR would not have jurisdiction over a refugee population which already had an existing agency attached to it. The Arab envoys knew that the resettling of refugees would validate Israel's victory in the 1948 War and therefore its existence as a state. It would also stop the flow of money to a population of people within their borders, meaning these leaders would have to care for the Palestinian refugees themselves. [256]

UNRWA Expands the Definition of the Refugee

In 1961, UNRWA voted to expand their definition of "Palestinian refugee," once defined as, "persons whose normal place of residence was Palestine during the period 1 June 1946 to 15 May 1948," to, "the descendants of Palestine refugees, including adopted children, are also eligible for registration."[257] This means that if normal international standards applied to all refugees listed by UNRWA, only 5% would be actual refugees. If those 5% had been resettled, like all other refugees, then there would be zero Palestinian refugees. But thanks to this expanded definition of refugee by UNRWA, the Palestinians are the only population of people who are considered refugees nearly one hundred years after a war that resulted in their displacement, and whose descendants are considered refugees regardless of how many generations have passed and which countries they now live in.

UNHCR

V.S.

UNRWA

Founded after WWII
Mission: Aid and protect
ALL refugees around the world
Staff: 18,000
Ratio of Staff per refugee:
1/1666
Resettled Refugees:

30 MILLION

Founded after WWII
Mission: Aid and protect
Palestinian Refugees ONLY
Staff: 30,000
Ratio of Staff per refugee:
1/193
Resettled Refugees:

ZERO

THE TALE OF TWO REFUGEE AGENCIES:

The UNHCR serves all refugees from all over the world and has resettled 30 million refugees, while UNRWA only serves Arab Palestinian refugees, but has resettled 0 refugees. The UNHCR has a staff of 20,305 (fluctuating by year,)[258] the equivalent of one staff member per 1,666 refugees, while UNRWA has a staff of 30,000, the equivalent of one staff member per 193 refugees.[259] In 2016, UNRWA's financial report stated the organization spent an average of 246 USD for each of the Palestinians it defines as a refugee.[260] In contrast, the UNHCR spends only a quarter of that: $47 per refugee.[261] Also important to note is that while the UNHCR staff is generally foreign, based primarily in Europe, UNRWA'S staff is almost entirely Palestinian. The organization is composed of Palestinians, exclusively operating in service of Palestinians.

THE UNRWA FORMULA

Every time a new refugee is added to UNRWA's jurisdiction, UNRWA gets more money from the international community. This is how it works: when refugee rolls grow, UNRWA tells its donor countries in the international community that more funds are needed to establish schools, hospitals, and vocational training in the West Bank and Gaza or in refugee camps in Jordan and Lebanon. The more money UNRWA claims to need, the more can be siphoned off to not provide for the Palestinian people, but to line the pockets of Palestinian "leaders." Remember, a large number of Palestinian refugees do not even live in the West Bank or Gaza, nor do they even live in Jordanian and Lebanese camps. Instead, they are middle-class businessmen in Dubai or law partners in Amman. This is how UNRWA engages in a spectacular kind of fraud.

Perspective: UNRWA vs. The Marshall Plan

The Marshall Plan was a grand effort initiated by the **Truman Administration** to distribute aid to post-war Europe from 1948 to 1951. In 2002 numbers, the United States distributed 60 billion USD to Europe over the course of the Marshall Plan, about 272 USD per European citizen. In contrast, from the period of the Oslo Accords to 2002, the Palestinians received 4 billion USD in total, rounding to 1,330 USD per Palestinian. In other words, Palestinians received more than four times the amount of money that European nations received after near total destruction, and still, the fundamental components of a state and successful society are missing in Palestinian society.[262]

The Right of Return

United Nations Resolution 194 states that, "refugees wishing to return to their homes and live at peace with their neighbors should be permitted to do so at the earliest practicable date."[263] UNRWA insists that this resolution means that Palestinians refugees from the 1948 War and their descendants have the right to return to the land a specific family member was displaced from within Israel's borders. Legal experts agree that Resolution 194 applies to individuals, not to entire peoples. Most importantly, the United Nations does not have the power or authority to establish a state's immigration policy, nor does Resolution 194 allow people who were never citizens of a newly established country to violate its sovereignty, which hundreds of thousands, if not millions, of Palestinians in Israel would surely do.

THE NAKBA

The term "Nakba" is Arabic for "catastrophe," coined by Syrian academic **Constantin Zureiq** in 1948 to criticize the *impotence* of the Egyptian, Jordanian, and Syrian armies in failing to defeat Israel.[264] Only later did Palestinian leadership claim that the Nakba/ Catastrophe referred to the flight of refugees during the 1948 war. The exodus of Palestinian Arabs, a comparably minor population movement in the 20th century, was exacerbated because no surrounding countries would absorb them, nor did they establish a state of their own. On the contrary, they repeatedly rejected one. The Palestinian claim to a right of return, seventy-five years after the war they lost, "the Nakba," is an unheard of concept in the history of warfare. This would be akin to England demanding that America give back its states because they didn't agree with the outcome in the revolutionary war. Most Arab Palestinians left at the urging of the surrounding Arab leaders, and some also fled at the outbreak of violence. Only a minority were expelled from their villages in the midst of Israeli military operations when they needed resources and land in order to defend their newly declared Jewish state. Today, the commemoration of the Nakba transparently attempts to falsely equate the plight of the Palestinians in 1948 to the Nazi genocide against the Jews, and to portray Israeli Jews as the new, modern day Nazis, a modern phenomenon called **Holocaust envy.**[265]

UNRWA'S Complicity with Terrorism

The October 7th massacre exposed the fact that dozens of individuals on the UNRWA payroll participated in the mass murder of Israeli civilians. Roughly 10% of UNRWA's Gaza staff had direct links to Hamas[266], and vast Hamas infrastructure operated under the UNRWA's headquarters in Gaza City. For ten months, UNRWA denied the evidence of internal cooperation with Hamas. In July 2024, UNRWA dismissed nine humanitarian aid workers for their involvement in the October 7th Massacre after international pressure.[267] In October of 2024, UNRWA confirmed that the head of Hamas operations in Lebanon, Fatah Sherif, was in fact an UNRWA employee, and at the time of his assassination in Israel was being "probed for his political activity."[268] In October of 2024, UNRWA confirmed that one of its employees, Mohammed Abu Attawi, was also a top commander of Hamas, who personally led the killing and kidnapping of Israelis from a roadside bomb shelter near Kibbutz Re'im on October 7th. The agency did not take action against Attawi, even though they were presented with evidence that he was a senior member of Hamas's terrorist operation.[269] It has since dawned on many that the Palestinian refugee status itself is a corrupt way to procure funds from the international community.

As of May 2024, the United States has frozen its funds to UNRWA, which averaged 350 million USD a year, increasing each year as the amount of refugees increased. Other states whose yearly contributions to the UNRWA remain frozen include the Netherlands (21.2 million USD), Italy (18 million USD), Austria (8.1 million USD), New Zealand (560K USD), Romania (210K USD), and Estonia (90K USD). Germany suspended its funding to the UNRWA (220 million USD) in October of 2023, but reinstated in April. Sweden (61 million USD), Japan (30 million

USD), France (28 million USD), Switzerland (25.5 million USD), Canada (23 million USD), Australia (13.8 million USD), the European Union (11.4 million USD), Finland (7.8 million USD), Iceland (558K USD) pulled their funding from the UNRWA at the outbreak of war against Hamas but, like Germany, reinstated it shortly thereafter.[270] As the exposure of UNRWA as a fraudulent terrorist entity becomes more evident, calls for its dismantling get louder.

How UNRWA Prevents a Palestinian State
Defenders of UNRWA often claim that the organization provides crucial services to the Palestinians, and that defunding UNRWA would leave Palestinians even more impoverished and ill-resourced. However, services that UNRWA provides – healthcare and education – are the normal responsibilities of a state, not a United Nations agency. By allowing UNRWA to perform state functions instead of elected Palestinian leaders, Palestinian sovereignty is kept in perpetual limbo. UNRWA leaders would rather keep the Palestinians stateless, enriching themselves with international aid, than to seriously negotiate with Israel to establish an independent state of Palestine. In doing so, UNRWA creates a new class of permanent refugees. UNRWA is financially incentivized to never resettle the Palestinians – never work to provide them a state of their own – and politically incentivized as well, as the organization's reason for existing is the eradication of a Jewish state in any borders. The Palestinian refugees are viewed as a perpetual battering ram against Jewish independence.

THE LEADERS WHO'VE BENEFITED

The leaders of Palestinian society are engaged in a form of thievery. What are they stealing? The resources, livelihoods, and future of their own people. Palestinian leaders have become enormously wealthy through the weaponization of the Israeli-Palestinian conflict.

Yassar Arafat, Founder of PLO 1929 - 2004

At the time of his death, Yasser Arafat, the founder of the Palestinian Liberation Organization (See: *The Big O*), boasted a net worth of an estimated 1.3 billion USD, of which an investigation by the International Monetary Fund (IMF) found over 900 million USD diverted to a privately controlled trust-fund during the years of peace negotiations with Israel.[271] Today, Arafat's children, who do not live in the Palestinian territories (and do not speak fluent Arabic), live lives of luxury in European palazzos. Arafat's daughter, Zahwa, was born in France and (reportedly) owns a street in London.[272] Arafat is only the beginning of the Palestinian corruption story. PLO officials have acquired fabulous wealth in the last few decades since the 1992 Oslo Accords, when money began pouring into the newly founded Palestinian Authority in much larger numbers. Since the '90s, PLO officials have built villas and spent millions on luxury cars[273] – while the citizens and countrymen in their midst suffer. Recent polls show 83% of the Palestinian people believe their government is corrupt.[274]

Mahmoud Abbas Palestinian Authority Leader 1935 -

As of this writing, the eighty-eight year old **Mahmood Abbas**, the anointed successor after Arafat's death in 2004, holds the position of President of the Palestinian Authority and the political party Fatah. Since Fatah lost the Palestinian Civil War for control of the Gaza Strip, Abbas hasn't held a single election in the Palestinian Authority-controlled West Bank for fear of losing there too. In 2020, news agencies revealed major corruption and siphoning of funds from international organizations on behalf of the Palestinian Authority.[275] Abbas owns several airplanes[276], a villa worth 13 million USD in the West Bank which he refers to as the "presidential palace,"[277] and as of 2024, has a net worth estimated at 100 million USD.[278]

HAMAS LEADERS: SINWAR AND HANIYEH

Before October 7th, Hamas had received more than 100 million USD in annual funding from Qatar and the Islamic Republic of Iran. They also received hundreds of millions annually from taxation on all smuggled products and evaded sanctions by using cryptocurrency.[279] NBC estimates that Hamas leadership has acquired at least 500 million USD in real estate and other assets.[280] Until their recent elimination, they lived lives of luxury in Qatar and their children received top education at Western universities, even though the people of Gaza suffer – with more than 47% reported to be unemployed.

Yahya Sinwar (1962- 2024)
During the most recent war, Hamas was politically and militarily led by **Yahya Sinwar**, following the assassination of Ismail Haniyeh in July 2024, the former political leader of the terror group.[281] Yahya Sinwar was also a millionaire. In 2023, the IDF discovered Hamas-run tunnels under Sinwar's various vacation homes.[282] In October of 2024, after Yahya Sinwar's elimination by the IDF, the passport of an UNRWA worker was discovered in his pocket.[283]

Ismail Haniyeh (1964 - 2024)

The former political leader of Hamas, **Ismail Haniyeh**, who was assassinated by the Mossad in Iran's capital of Tehran a few months before this book was published, was a billionaire living a life of luxury in Qatar before his death (the networth for Hamas leaders living in Qatar is estimated to be approximately 11 billion USD)[284] Haniyeh's oldest son was arrested in 2014 for smuggling millions of USD worth of goods from Egypt into the southern Gazan city of **Rafah**.[285] Haniyeh also notably owned various mansions in Gaza, all listed under his childrens' names to avoid political repercussions from Gazans.[286]

LANGUAGE IS IMPORTANT: "REFUGEE CAMP"

A **refugee camp** in Gaza is simply a regular town with apartment buildings, stores, shopping malls, etc. It looks like other cities. It is still called a refugee camp because the initial population of the neighborhood consisted of people who arrived during the 1948 War when the local Arabs and surrounding Arab countries invaded Israel. As stated above, by calling regular neighborhoods refugee camps, leaders can continue to receive and siphon off donations from the international community.

PALESTINIAN INDOCTRINATION

In addition to creating a perpetual flow of money for its leaders, UNRWA teachers indoctrinate children from a tender age in both the West Bank and the Gaza Strip, creating and distributing curriculum rife with antisemitic tropes and hateful incitement against Israelis.[287] This indoctrination has the immediate effect of radicalization. Palestinian textbooks call for jihad (holy war) against civilians as well as martyrdom – committing the noble act of dying in service of the war against the Jews.[288] Over seventy Palestinian schools in Gaza and the West Bank are named after terrorists, including Nazi collaborators.[289] As recently as 2023, Hamas ran summer camps in Gaza, attended by more than 100,000 children, which teach jihad and martyrdom in the service of a Palestine free "from the river to the sea."[290] Children learn how to use weapons, including knives and firearms, and even practice hand-to-hand combat.[291] Long before the October 7th Massacre, journalists reported childrens' plays glorifying the killing of Jews and taking of Israeli hostages.

1972: THE MUNICH MASSACRE

The UNRWA school system produced the Palestinian terrorists who murdered eleven Israelis at the **Olympic Games in Munich, Germany**. At the time, Germans had kept security lax to prove that their country was no longer the dangerous and authoritarian Nazi state it used to be. Eight Palestinian militants from the terror group Black September, assisted and abetted by German Neo-Nazis, invaded the living quarters of the athletes in the Olympic villages, killed their coaches, and took the Israelis hostage, demanding the release of Palestinians serving prison sentences for acts of violence in Israel.[292] Attempts to rescue them failed and all the hostages were shot and killed.

HAMAS' TERROR TUNNELS

Until Israel declared war on Gaza after the October 7th Massacre, the world was mostly unaware that Hamas really fired rockets from hospitals and kindergartens.[293] The extent of Hamas's underground complexes, lying beneath countless residential areas in the Gaza Strip, shocked the world. The over 300 miles of **tunnels** were more extensive and a longer system than the Paris Metro and the London Tube combined.[294] The tunnels are not used to protect the civilian population of Gaza, rather to shield Hamas's leaders and to store weapons caches and fighters.[295] The billions of USD in international aid, including approximately 1.49 billion USD in cash from Qatar between 2012 and 2021, slated for schools and hospitals, instead went to building tunnels and carrying out terrorist attacks, as well as into the bank accounts of Hamas leaders.[296] UNRWA's funding also contributes: before the war, a photo of UNRWA-produced bags of food were used to pad an entrance to a Hamas-run tunnel went viral.[297] Gaza has received over 40 billion USD in aid from 1994 to 2000, and produced close to no state infrastructure for the Palestinians aside from these tunnels.[298]

HAMAS' BLACKMAIL & PERMIT ABUSE

We covered how the Palestinian Authority abuses work permits in the West Bank, and the same holds true for Gazans prior to the most recent war. Thousands of Palestinians are granted permits to enter Israel for medical needs on a regular basis. Hamas repeatedly blackmailed these Palestinians, withholding permits to them on the condition that they do Hamas's bidding: delivering messages or funds to and from the West Bank and other parts of the Middle East.[299] Hamas also bribes Palestinians in Gaza with small amounts of cash for engaging in acts of terror against Israel, such as in the Gaza border riots in 2018-2019, promising them more money if they were injured, provoking the police and army.[300]

PAY FOR SLAY

The Palestinian Authority in the West Bank has an entire ministry dedicated to depositing money into the bank accounts of terrorists serving time in Israeli prison for attacks against Israelis and also family members of terrorists, which they call the **Martyrs Fund**[301], which is also known in the West as **Pay for Slay**. The Martyrs Fund has a sliding pay scale based on the status of the terrorist (married, children, etc.) and even pays extra if the terrorist holds Israeli citizenship. The longer one serves in jail, the more money the family will get. Multiple sources show that between $150 million and $300 million are spent each year paying these terrorists and their families.[302]

DR. EINAT WILF

Einat Wilf is a former member of Knesset from the Labor Party and is now considered to be one of the most articulate spokespeople for Israel and Jews. Beginning her career as an advocate for the Israeli left and the Oslo peace process, Dr. Wilf became disillusioned with the "land for peace" formula after the Second Intifada, and turned her focus toward examining the goals of Palestinian society. She co-authored *The War of Return: How Western Indulgence in the Palestinian Dream Has Obstructed the Path to Peace* with fellow scholar Adi Schwartz – a book that exposed the corruption of UNRWA and the lie of the Palestinian refugee crisis in detail.

Pay for Slay *(cont.)*

Among those killed by these terrorists are 69 Americans.[303] In 2018, the Trump Administration signed the **Taylor Force Act**, named after a Texan soldier who was killed in the line of duty, which conditions that no economic aid to the Palestinian Authority be used to pay off terrorists and their families, and the payments were stopped.[304] In response to criticism over Pay for Slay, President Mahmoud Abbas famously declared, "Even if I will have to leave my position, I will not compromise on the salary (rawatib) of a Martyr (Shahid) or a prisoner."[305] In 2021 the Biden administration resumed payments in violation of the Taylor Force Act but then stopped shortly after Oct 7th.[306] The future of aid to the Palestinian Authority and UNRWA is unclear.

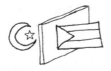

ARAB APARTHEID AGAINST PALESTINIANS

It is ironic that Israel, which has a roughly 20% Arab Palestinian population, all of whom enjoy equal rights with the rest of the Jewish population, is accused of apartheid, when it is the surrounding Arab nations who treat Arab Palestinians in a discriminatory manner. Beginning with the assassination of King Abdullah of Jordan in 1951, all the Arab states surrounding Israel have opposed settling Palestinians within their borders, thereby encouraging permanent Palestinian refugee status.[307] To preserve the conflict, throughout the 1950s, the **Arab League**, an assembly of Arab nations established to supposedly further the interests of Arab peoples (but only served to propagate hatred and blame against Israel),[308] passed multiple resolutions to rescind prior citizenship offers to Palestinians, and to prohibit any permanent resettlement efforts of refugees in Jordan, Egypt, Lebanon, Syria, or Saudi Arabia.[309] This has led to apartheid-style laws for Palestinians in these countries.

For example, in Lebanon, the majority of Palestinians live in criminally underfunded neighborhoods and are barred from practicing law or medicine or owning land.[310] In Egypt, Palestinians are denied rights afforded to other citizens, including free education and healthcare.[311] Palestinians face severe restrictions on workers rights and privileges. In Jordan, where Palestinians comprise roughly 70% of the population, they are underrepresented in government and have quotas for limiting university attendance. Furthermore, Jordanian based Palestinian refugees don't have the same free education and healthcare as other citizens and are barred from practicing law or becoming an engineer.[312] Palestinian refugees in Syria are completely dependent on UNRWA support for housing, healthcare, and education.[313] The Syrian government refuses to accommodate the close to half a million Palestinians in its borders.

Apartheid Against Palestinians *(cont.)*

Even more glaring, since the October 7th Massacre, not a single Arab country has taken in one Palestinian refugee from the Gaza Strip.[314] In contrast, when Russia invaded Ukraine in 2022, millions of Ukrainians fled for Poland, Western Europe, and even the United States.[315] When Assad started the civil war in Syria, Germany took in over 1 million refugees.[316] Arab countries, by contrast, fear that a large influx of a radicalized Palestinian population would lead to terrorism.

PALESTINIAN INCITEMENT

A staple of Palestinian leadership since its inception has been the incitement to violence and terrorism. Streets, public squares, and schools in the West Bank and Gaza Strip are named after Palestinian suicide bombers and terrorists such as **Leila Khaled**, who hijacked a commercial flight in an act of terrorism.[317] Palestinian media is permeated with glorification of "martyrs" (terrorists).[318] Even children's shows and school plays are often reenactments of terror attacks or the slaughter of Israelis.[319] Arabic social media glorifies Palestinian acts of egregious violence, including the gunning down of Israeli Jews during Shabbat services.

THE MYTH OF STORMING THE AL-AQSA MOSQUE

In 1929, Arabs ethnically cleansed the Jews from the city of Hebron in an event known as the **Hebron Massacre**, fueled by the (false) rumor that the Jews were imminently going to destroy Al-Aqsa Mosque (Jerusalem and Safed were also brutally attacked that year.)[320] The mob, incited by the Mufti of Jerusalem Haj Amin al-Hussein, unfurled a murderous rampage against local Jewish communities. The same rumor of Jews planning to storm Al-Aqsa Mosque launched a wave of terrorism known as the Second Intifada.[321] Every year during Ramadan, Palestinian leaders falsely claim Al-Aqsa is in danger, inciting religious extremists to take up arms and murder innocent Jewish people. This triggered the 2021 war between Israel and Hamas, known to Israelis as Operation "Guardian of the Walls."[322] Despite these rumors, the reality is that Israel guarantees freedom of worship for any Muslims who wish to pray at the Al-Aqsa Mosque, and the mosque has never been in danger of destruction.

PALESTINIANS vs. N. & S. KOREA

For perspective, the 3.1 million Korean refugees born from the Korean War were settled in a span of three years, all while using a third of UNRWA's budget.[323] South Korea was an absolute wasteland in the 1950s, but today, boasts the beautiful cosmopolitan city of Seoul, a booming economy, and a thriving democracy. We do not see South Koreans staring across the 38th parallel, the border between North and South Korea, seething, planning warfare against Kim Jong-Un for the sake of returning home. Instead, South Koreans turned their lot into an incredibly prosperous and successful present and optimistic future, what the Palestinians and the Arab world could have easily accomplished in the West Bank and Gaza should they have recognized Israel's right to exist. But, unfortunately, the Palestinian vision of return and revenge prevents any forward movement in the conflict, and this is legitimized and validated by the letters "UN" found in UNRWA.

THE WORLD IS WAKING UP

In October of 2024, Israel's Knesset passed two bills outlawing UNRWA from operating within Israeli territory, including East Jerusalem, and forbade any Israeli from cooperating with the organization, including the IDF.[324] As UNRWA's collaboration with Hamas and the forever war against Israel becomes clear, more and more countries are disassociating and reexamining their support of this organization.

6

THE
UNITED NATIONS

On November 28, 1947, thousands gathered around their radios as, one by one, member states of the **United Nations General Assembly (UNGA)** voted to approve the creation of the Jewish state of Israel. Jews danced in the streets of Jerusalem for hours on end, celebrating, at long last, the re-establishment of their country. The events leading up to the vote required a collective awakening among the Jewish people, expert statecraft, and timing: when empires were falling in the aftermath of World War II and many new states were rising from the ashes. Israel became a nation in 1948 and shares its birth year with Myanmar and North and South Korea. India and Pakistan were born a year earlier in 1947, Jordan and the Philippines in 1946.

It is a misconception that Israel was created as a response to the Holocaust. In fact, because of the six million Jews who were murdered by the Nazis, many thought there might not be enough people to constitute a Jewish state. In the case of Israel's birth, the powers and authority of the United Nations were used for good. Unfortunately, the original intentions of the institution have strayed significantly since its early days, making the world a more dangerous place.

UN ORIGINS AND HISTORY

Established in 1945 at the end of World War II, the United Nations represented a beacon of hope; a forum where reasonable nations would talk instead of going to war. Dozens of countries had just experienced a loss of life so dramatic and violent that many believed a forum where various nations could vote on resolutions concerning human rights, economics, trade, resources, and conflict, could hasten world peace. The **United Nations Charter** prioritizes the pursuit of peace and security for every country in the world, commits to combating world hunger, disease and illiteracy, the development of resource-deprived areas, and the adherence of all member states to international law. All member states of the United Nations make legally-binding declarations accepting these obligations.[325]

The UN has six principal organs which include: The General Assembly (UNGA), the **Security Council (UNSC)**, the Economic and Social Council (ECOSOC), the Trusteeship Council, the International Court of Justice (ICJ), and the UN Secretariat.

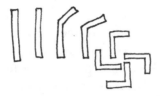

KEY EVENTS OF THE UNITED NATIONS GENERAL ASSEMBLY (UNGA)

The United Nations General Assembly currently comprises 193 member states (countries), and each state's vote has equal representation and equal weight. Here is a brief timeline of their achievements and an illustration to see how far they've fallen as it relates to Israel.

1949: Res. 273 - Israel Revives a Nation

The General Assembly votes and officially grants Israel member status voting with 37 states for, 12 against, 9 abstaining.[326]

1975-1991 Res. 3379 Russia: "Zionism = Racism"

Although there are Christian, Hindu, and Muslim countries, in 1975 the Soviet Union attempted to label Zionism, and therefore Israel, a racist enterprise. After a series of intense debates, the United Nations General Assembly adopted **Resolution 3379** (72 voted for, 35 against, 32 abstained), proposed by the Soviet Union and intensely supported by the Arab states of the Middle East, which designated Zionism "as a form of racism and racial discrimination."[327] **Daniel Patrick Moynihan**, then the U.S. Ambassador to the United Nations, called 3379's passing "a moment of infamy."[328] Israeli Ambassador Haim Herzog tore up the paper resolution during his formal address in response. Though repealed in 1991, Resolution 3379 and its hateful legacy persists today.

2001: The Durban Conference - Antisemitism Emerges in Full Force

After the fall of the racist apartheid system in South Africa, **Durban** emerged as the new capital of anti-racism and human rights, making it the perfect setting for the opening of the General Assembly. But in September of 2001, days before the 9/11 terrorist attacks in America, an antisemitic hate-fest commenced during the supposed celebration of international cooperation. Instigators distributed **Adolf Hitler**'s memoir, *Mein Kampf*, along with cartoons of Jews with hooked noses and beady eyes. Protestors on the streets shouted "Zionism is Nazism." Speakers including Yasser Arafat and Fidel Castro, the communist dictator of Cuba, called for boycotting the Jewish state. Jewish and Israeli participants left the conference early distraught, but UNGA's disproportionate focus on Israel was just beginning.[329]

WHY IS UNGA SO OBSESSED WITH ISRAEL?

In 2020, at the height of the pandemic, when global cooperation over medicine and trade was of the utmost importance, the UNGA passed seventeen resolutions against Israel versus just six for every other country- combined. In 2022, the UNGA passed more resolutions condemning the State of Israel than against Russia, China, Saudi Arabia, and other oppressive regimes – combined.[330] Since the October 7th Massacre of 2023 by Hamas, the impulse to condemn Israel fiercely continues. On October

27th and December 31st of 2023, the UNGA overwhelmingly passed resolutions calling for a ceasefire to the war in Gaza without mentioning the terrorist organization of Hamas once.[331]

Why this bias against and obsession with Israel? By using Israel as a scapegoat, states with the worst human rights records deflect and divert attention from themselves. What are some examples of those wrongdoings? There are almost too many to list, but we can try:

The Islamic Republic of Iran

Iran was a founding member of the United Nations before becoming an Islamist state, granting it special privileges afforded to all original members. But since the Islamic Revolution in 1979, the Islamic Republic has used the UN to aid its efforts to export terrorism throughout the Middle East and the world. In 2024, while the world held its breath in fear of Iran achieving its goal of creating a nuclear bomb, the Islamic Republic of Iran actually served as the chair of the United Nations Conference on Disarmament.[332] Until 2022, after global outrage ended that appointment, Iran served on the **UN Commission on the Status of Women**, despite the country's policy of forcing women to cover their hair and neck (or be severely punished, beaten, blinded, disappeared, murdered by the "Morality Police.")[333] The Islamic Republic continues to commit egregious human rights abuses including violently criminalizing freedom of expression, discriminating against religious and ethnic minorities, and leading the world in the number of known executions of civilians. These violations receive few, if any, UNGA condemnations.

China

The UNGA has yet to take a strong, definitive stance against China's treatment of its **Uighur Muslim minority** who are put in concentration camp-like facilities for the purpose of "re-education" and forced labor.[334] Nor has the UNGA mentioned China's use of mass surveillance to monitor its population and to restrict, in many ways, freedom of speech and expression.[335] China scored a 9 out of 100 in the annual **Freedom House** report, which ranks political and personal liberties in each country. By contrast, Israel earned a 74.[336]

Russia

The UNGA has condemned the inhumane war against Ukraine, but since Russia, another founding member, has **veto power** over the UN Security Council, all such pronouncements are toothless. Furthermore, the UNGA has made no mention of the fact that Putin's Russia has become a world capital for the criminalization of free speech and expression, including independent journalism. Nor has it reflected on the commonly improbable unanimous election results or the regular poisoning, disappearance, or imprisonment of political opponents (most recently **Alexei Navalny**). Russia has also contributed to such conflicts as the Syrian Civil War, where hundreds of thousands of civilians, including Palestinians, were targeted and killed by Bashar al-Assad.[337]

North Korea, and Others

Many other countries around the globe, including the authoritarian regime of North Korea, the genocidal state-run militias of Myanmar, the corrupt kleptocracies of Latin America, and the warring nations of Africa, fall drastically below Israel when it comes to protection of human rights. These nations cannot be conceived of, by any stretch of the imagination, as democracies. And yet, they receive almost mention from the UN General Assembly. With this in mind, it's hard to arrive at a different conclusion than, "Don't look at me, look at..." or rather, "...blame...": Israel. This double standard becomes especially stark when you consider casualties of all other conflicts compared to the casualties of all of Israel's conflicts combined:

DEATH TOLLS OF MAJOR CONFLICTS IN THE LAST 100 YEARS

Conflict	Death Tolls
Afghan War 2000 -2021	250,000[338]
Iran-Iraq War 1980-1988	~1,000,000[339]
Syrian Civil War 2011-Present	300,000~500,000[340]
Somali Civil War 1991--Present	~500,000[341]
Yemen Civil War 2014-Present	~377,000[342]
Darfur 2003-2020	~300,000[343]
Russo-Ukraine War 2021 - Present	~1,000,000+
Israel-Palistinian Conflict[344] **1967- Oct 7, 2023 (both sides)**	~40,500[345]

ABBA EBEN

If Algeria introduced a resolution declaring that the earth was flat and that Israel had flattened it, it would pass by a vote of 164 to 13 with 26 abstentions.

-Abba Eben, Israel's first Ambassador to the United Nations

UNSC

THE UNITED NATIONS SECURITY COUNCIL

The stated mission of the **United Nations Security Council (UNSC)** is to protect global stability and avoid conflict. The five permanent, veto-wielding founding members include the United States, France, the United Kingdom, China, and Russia. A variety of rotating members are elected for a term of two years. Countries often team up and make deals in order to conceal acts worthy of condemnation, such as the invasion of Ukraine, or to deflect from the wrongdoings of Iran. Israel regularly relies upon America's veto power to stop the incessant scurrilous anti-Israel resolutions.

THE UNITED NATIONS EDUCATIONAL, SCIENTIFIC, AND CULTURAL ORGANIZATION

The **United Nations Educational, Scientific, and Cultural Organization's (UNESCO)** mission is to preserve cultural heritage and history worldwide but instead continually denies and downplays Jewish history and connection in the land and peddles in narratives designed to undermine Jewish history in the region. Iran and other regimes, eager to keep the focus on the Palestinian conflict lest scrutiny gaze upon their own human rights violations, actively use international bodies like the UN as a political football field to advance resolutions against Israel. Anti-Israel resolutions contribute to an atmosphere of mistrust and make it more challenging to find common ground for negotiations. UNESCO resolutions designed to undermine Israel and the Jews include:

Cave of the Patriarchs and Rachel's Tomb

In 2010, UNESCO passed a resolution referring to the Cave of the Patriarchs in Hebron as solely Palestinian, though the site is also holy to Jews,[346] and to **Rachel's Tomb** in Bethlehem as the "Bilal bin Rabah Mosque/Rachel's Tomb," even though the **Bilal bin Rabah Mosque** had only been used as a name for the Jewish holy site since Palestinian anti-Israel riots in 1996.[347] Both sites are sacred to Jews and predate Islam by millennia, yet UNESCO overlooked this fact and used politically charged language to construct a false narrative.

RACHEL'S TOMB

Western Wall and the Dome of the Rock

In 2016, UNESCO passed a resolution referring to the Western Wall, one of the holiest sites in Judaism, only by its Arabic name, **Al-Buraq Plaza**, and claimed that it was part of the "Al-Aqsa Mosque compound." The resolution also includes a condemnation of "right-wing Israelis" who were "denying freedom of worship and Muslims' access to their holy sites," and "the continuous storming of Al-Aqsa Mosque."[348] As Israeli professor Shany Mor has written extensively on, the claim that the Al-Aqsa Mosque is in danger is an antisemitic libel that has been used to stir up violence against Jews in the Middle East for centuries.[349]

The Old City of Jerusalem

In 2017, UNESCO again adopted a resolution that referred to the Temple Mount, the holiest site in Judaism which existed long before Al-Aqsa Mosque, solely by its Arabic name, **Al-Haram Al-Sharif**. Submitted to UNESCO's Executive Board by Algeria, Egypt, Lebanon, Morocco, Oman, Qatar and Sudan, the resolution on "Occupied Palestine," indicated that Israel had no legal or historical rights anywhere in Jerusalem. The resolution passed with 22 countries in favor, 23 abstentions, 10 opposed, and the representatives of three countries absent.[350]

The U.S. withdrew from UNESCO on account of its anti-Israel bias in 2019, but rejoined in 2023. Those in favor of the decision claimed it would delegitimize the corrupt institution, while others claimed that the U.S.'s presence on the council is necessary to fight against Israel-bias.[351]

HEROES: HILLEL NEUER - UN WATCH

Hillel Neuer is the executive director of **UN Watch**, an NGO with the mission statement of addressing and combating anti-Israel bias at the UN and the excusing of crimes against humanity by authoritarian regimes. Neuer has been instrumental in bringing attention to the grift perpetuated by UNRWA, as well as the funneling of U.S. taxpayer money to build Hamas's tunnels and pay the salaries of terrorists. In 2023, UN Watch revealed that more than 3,000 UNRWA teachers had celebrated the October 7th Massacre in online group chats.[352]

UNITED NATIONS HUMAN RIGHTS COUNCIL

The UN Human Rights Council (UNHRC)'s purported goal is to promote "universal respect for the protection of all human rights and fundamental freedoms for all" and to address all human rights violations, sudden and systemic. If only that were true. More than half of the council's membership are theocrats and dictators of regimes committing the worst offenses. This body currently includes: Cuba, which arbitrarily executes and tortures political dissidents;[353] Sudan, where millions of people have been displaced due to ongoing war featuring child soldiers;[354] and Bangladesh, whose culture brandishes extreme gender inequality and corruption.[355] Other current members of the UNHRC include Qatar, China, Eritrea, Algeria, Kuwait, Burundi, Somalia, Vietnam, and Kazakhstan.[356]

The UNHRC's Bias Against Israel
The United Nations Human Rights Council is the most openly antagonistic against Israel of all UN bodies, likely because its resolutions are not legally binding and therefore subjected to less scrutiny. As of 2013, Israel had been condemned 45 times, accounting for almost 50% of all country-specific resolutions passed by the council in the same time frame.[357] Israel is the only nation in the entire world subjected to a permanent agenda item in every session of the UNHCR – Agenda Item 7.[358] The Council's anti-Israel bias is so pronounced that the U.S. refuses to participate in Agenda Item 7 as a matter of course.[359]

Since the outbreak of the October 7th War, the UNHRC has repeatedly called for an immediate ceasefire to hostilities, has curiously called on any neighboring states to not allow for the relocation of Palestinians in Gaza to protect them, and has demanded that UN member states stop the shipment of arms to Israel.[360] In April 2024, the UNHRC condemned Israel for its war against Hamas, but made no mention of Hamas nor the atrocities committed on October 7th.[361]

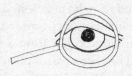

UN SPECIAL RAPPORTEUR TO THE OCCUPIED PALESTINIAN TERRITORIES

After the Oslo Accords in 1993, the UN established a new, supposedly impartial position of the Special Rapporteur to the Occupied Palestinians Territories, tasked with reporting on the human rights situation for Palestinians in the West Bank in Gaza. The position has repeatedly been filled by notoriously anti-Israel and some antisemitic academics such as Richard Falk,[362] and more recently **Francesca Albanese**. Albanese regularly accuses Israel of genocide and denies Israel's right to self-defense in response to the attacks by Hamas whom she refuses to condemn. Albanese has claimed that there was no evidence of rape as a method of war on October 7th, despite even the UN's begrudging and belated acknowledgement of such assaults.[363]

INTERNATIONAL COURT OF JUSTICE

The International Court of Justice (ICJ) is a branch of the UN which handles non-political disputes between nations and provides advisory opinions on international legal issues. It is composed of fifteen judges who are elected by both the General Assembly and the Security Council and who serve for a term of nine years, with each judge being from a separate nationality. Unfortunately, the ICJ has been weaponized as a political tool to manipulate international law. Let's take a look at South Africa:

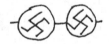

South Africa's "Case" Against Israel (Durban 2.0)

In 2023-2024, South Africa accused Israel of committing genocide during their war against Hamas in Gaza after the October 7th Massacre, taking them to the ICJ despite having no practical stake in the Israeli-Palestinian conflict. The legal definition of **genocide** was established by the UN as a response to the Holocaust, the Nazi genocide of the Jewish people,[364] making the accusation by South Africa all the more repugnant. In a series of dramatic hearings in December 2023, South Africa falsely claimed that Israel had gone out of its way to kill civilians in Gaza "with the intent to destroy part or all of an ethnic, racial, or religious population." The court did not agree that Israel was carrying out a genocide, nor did it order Israel to stop the war in Gaza against Hamas.[365] Indeed, Israel does not target civilians – its war in Gaza was launched as a defensive measure against a terrorist organization, not a civilian population.[366] In September of 2024, international media reported that South Africa is trying to extend the deadline for their proceedings against Israel at the International Court of Justice. The country is unable to prove its accusation of genocide with evidence.[367]

NGO Collusion with Terror Organizations

At face value, **Non-Governmental Organizations (NGOs)** are created to advance human rights, economic development, and diplomatic relations. Many NGOs partner within the United Nations. While these organizations can be forces for good, many fall prey to corruption due to lack of regulation and oversight. Some NGOs allow terrorist organizations to launder money and act as a cover for terrorist activities. Since the majority of Palestinian society has been indoctrinated to believe that Israel has no right to exist, multiple NGOs operating for and by the Palestinians foment rejectionism and violence and maintain ties to designated terrorist organizations. In 2021, the following organizations were found to have direct links with the **Popular Front for the Liberation of Palestine (PFLP)**,[368] a designated terrorist organization according to the U.S., the EU, Israel, and Canada:

- Union of Agricultural Work Committees (UAWC)
- The Defense for Children International-Palestine (DCI-P)
- Al-Haq, based in Ramallah to defend Palestinian human rights
- Addameer, monitoring Palestinian prisoner rights
- Union of Palestinian Women's Committees
- Bisan Center, supporting youth and women in civil society
- Health Work Committee (HWC)
- Palestinian Human Rights Association, also a designated terrorist organization

NGO Collusion with Terror Organizations *(cont.)*

Many members of NGOs are also members of terrorist organizations including the PFLP. In 2024, three NGO officials operating within Israel were indicted for their involvement in an August 2019 bombing that killed an Israeli teenager.[369] Thirty-seven additional NGO officials have direct connections with the PFLP. As of 2024, nine have been convicted for planning or executing other terrorist attacks. In 2022, the Dutch government identified 34 individuals from the UAWC and the PFLP between 2007 and 2020 which led to the Netherlands canceling its contract with the UAWC.[370] Since then, Citibank, Arab Bank, American Express, Visa, and Mastercard all shut down online donations to and the accounts of PFLP-linked NGOs.[371]

Should Terrorism Be Rewarded With Statehood?

In 2012, the Palestinian Authority petitioned the United Nations General Assembly for official statehood status and was accepted as an observer state that November, while still refusing to negotiate a political settlement with Israel. Following the October 7th Massacre, Palestinian leaders revived their petition to the UN for full statehood, using international sympathy for the people of Gaza as leverage. The United States vetoed the application in the UN Security Council. As of April 2024, 140 of 193 states have recognized the state of Palestine independently.[372]

7

LIES AND MISCONCEPTIONS

Antisemitism—often called the "world's oldest hatred"—is the most common term for the ever-evolving discrimination and demonization of Jewish people rooted in falsehoods. Unlike other forms of prejudice, antisemitism does not simply portray Jews as inferior; instead, it depicts them as possessing special powers or wielding secretive control and undue influence over society. This societal disease mutates with each era.

Antisemitism often requires the blessing of the highest authority of the era in order to become a popular movement. As an example, in the Middle Ages, when the Church believed that the Jews were committing the gravest transgression in not accepting Christ as the son of God, deadly riots against Jewish villages were sanctioned, simply because the Church said so. Only a few years after Galileo was sentenced to death by the Catholic Church for saying that the earth revolved around the sun, Europe entered the age of Enlightenment and religion became subservient to emerging scientific ideas about nationality and race. As a result, Jews were then perceived as foreigners instead of Christ-killers, trying to undermine the social order by way of democracy, capitalism, communism, and nationalism. Name any "ism" – the Jews are accused of being behind it.

Today, ideas of nationality and race are replaced with those of human rights, social justice, and liberation for the downtrodden. And this is how the "world's oldest hatred" mutates into "anti-Zionism." Israel, the "Jew among nations" is vilified as the ultimate oppressor of the oppressed, the epitome of racism, white supremacy, colonialism, and a host of other evils.

LANGUAGE IS IMPORTANT: "ANTISEMITISM"

The word antisemitism was coined by German journalist and previous communist activist **Wilhelm Marr** who claimed that the "Semitic race" was inferior to the **Aryan Race**. Marr's political organization, "The League of Antisemites," was popular in late nineteenth century Europe. This, despite the fact that "semitic" is a philological term referring to a school of languages, not a race.[373] If anything, the attempted slight of this word reveals that Jews have always been known to be from the Levant region, which is now Israel/Lebanon/Syria – and always seen as different. It's only in America in the late 20th and early 21st centuries that the Jewish people were ever considered "white."

ANTISEMITISM THROUGH THE AGES

The ultimate test of the success of any country or nation is whether or not it can tolerate a successful minority in its midst. If a society gets sick, they historically always come for the Jews first. Afterwards comes the other minorities. Jews are not special; they are often just first. Below is a brief overview of the starring role antisemitism has played in various societies who all, in the end, collapsed into the dustbin of history.

The Christians (500-1700s)
Christian Europe began with the fall of the Roman Empire in the 6th century, and ended with the Enlightenment (17th-18th century). In many ways, Jews thrived in this era by proving useful to Christians who were forbidden to handle money or trade directly with Muslim rulers overseas; Jews were not forbidden to handle money and so could serve as intermediaries. But Jews' usefulness only lasted for so long, for as soon as a powerful lord faced a crisis, of which there were many in this dangerous time, Jews were the perfect people to blame. The Church perpetuated lies which included that Jews killed Jesus Christ (it was the Romans), or that Jews killed Christian babies and used their blood to make matzah during the holiday of Passover (also known as the **blood libel.**) The masses were routinely encouraged to attack Jewish villages, sometimes killing in the thousands, and the status-quo continued.[374]

The Crusades (1000-1291)

In the High Middle Ages, European Christians attempted, multiple times, to conquer the Land of Israel, what they referred to simply as the "Holy Land," at the time under Muslim/Arab rule. In the midst of Christian invasions, the European public was captured by a sort of religious, messianic fervor, and massacred thousands of Jews in their midst, most commonly those living along the Rhineland in Germany and France. The Jewish communities of Speyer, Worms, and Mainz were also destroyed during the massacres. Thousands of Jews were killed in the Land of Israel as well, defending fortresses and lands from European Christians.[375]

The Spanish Inquisition

In 1478, **King Ferdinand II and Queen Isabella of Aragon** established the Spanish Inquisition, a program of political persecution against non-Catholics in Spain and later, in all Spanish territory overseas. In the pursuit of identifying heretics, thousands of Jews and Muslims were imprisoned, tortured, expelled, forcefully converted, and even executed, including Jews and Muslims who had already converted to Catholicism. The mass expulsion of Jews from Spain contributed to a large population of Sephardic Jews in North Africa and other parts of Europe. Many Jews today in Europe, North America, and Israel trace their lineage back to Spain or other parts of the Spanish Empire.[376]

The Russians (1700s-1917)

With the onset of the Enlightenment, the Industrial Revolution, and the invention of electricity and many types of machines, Europe faced many challenging questions, not unlike the tumult modern society faces in the wake of today's technological revolution. Nowhere was the social upheaval more prominent than in nearby Russia, where the masses finally began rebelling against the oppressive Czar, or Emperor. While chaos consumed Russia on its way to revolution, a fraudulent and horribly antisemitic document known as *The Protocols of the Elders of Zion* was published and serialized in a widely read Russian newspaper. While the exact origins of the Protocols are unknown, the book places the blame for all of the world's ills on a secret society of Jews, including the idea that Jews control the economy, the media, national conflicts, and anything requiring someone to blame. The Protocols led to, or provided justification for, an explosion of violence against Jews in Russia and was one of the biggest inspirations for Adolf Hitler and his Nazi Party. Sadly, these documents have been translated into Arabic and numerous other languages and are still widely circulated today.[377]

The Germans (1880s-1945)

German Romantic nationalism began in the 19th century when German intellectuals proposed that an independent German people, united by a common language and culture, were destined to build a great, sovereign country in the center of Europe. With German centrism, however, came antagonism toward minorities, particularly Jews – with many nationalists peddling in the belief that Jews soiled German culture, degrading what it meant to be German by way of their foreign religion and language, Yiddish, itself a combination of Hebrew and German. Things reached a climax in the humiliating German defeat in World War I, which left the German population poor, embarrassed, and looking for someone to blame.[378]

Adolf Hitler, a German ground soldier on the Western Front, became a popular name in right-wing circles against the newly formed **Weimar Republic**, which valued democracy, liberalism, and personal freedom. Hitler launched a failed coup in an attempt to overthrow the Weimar Republic in 1923, which earned him a prison sentence. In jail, he penned *Mein Kampf*, My Struggle. In this book, he accuses the Jews of destroying society: purposely conspiring to help the Allied Powers win World War I, bringing in communism to Germany, controlling the economy, and tainting what it meant to be of German "race."[379]

World War II and the Holocaust

After a series of failures by the liberals and socialists of the Weimar Republic to organize power in Germany, Hitler and his Nazi party, short for "National Socialists," seized power in the Reichstag, the German parliament, in 1933, and Hitler quickly became *Der Fuhrer*, the Supreme Leader, of Germany. Throughout the 1930s, the Nazis passed a series of discriminatory laws, coined the **Nuremberg Laws** which stripped Jews of their political rights, illegalized Jewish presence in public life and in public service, outlawed intermarriage between non-Jews and Jews, and eventually forced Jews to live only within certain areas of cities.[380]

When Germany invaded Poland, and World War II commenced, Nazi persecution against Jews became horrifically more extreme. Designated living zones of Jews, called ghettos, became filthy and rife with disease. Newly established Nazi squadrons, called the SS and the Gestapo, began systematically murdering Jews inside the ghettos themselves, or transporting them to newly established concentration camps, where Jews were often worked to death. These were the death camps where hundreds of thousands of Jews were killed in gas chambers upon arrival. Approximately one-million Jews were killed in the most infamous death camp: Auschwitz-Birkenau.[381] Another squadron within the Nazi army, the *Einsatzgruppen*, was tasked with following the German army as it invaded Eastern Europe and Russia, killing what's estimated to be upwards of one million Jews by way of firing squad, what came to be known as the "Holocaust by bullet."[382]

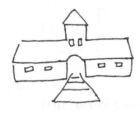

World War II and the Holocaust *(cont.)*

The destruction of European Jewry over the course of the Holocaust is the greatest crime ever recorded in history. Six million Jewish men, women, and children were either shot in fields or murdered in camps like **Auschwitz-Birkenau, Treblinka, Sobibor, and Bergen-Belsen**. They hailed from nearly every country in mainland Europe, including Poland, Russia, France, Italy, Hungary, Holland, Switzerland, and more. **Amos Elon**'s book, *The Pity of It All*, gives great insight into Germany's Jews leading up to the Holocaust, who were once considered model citizens. Indeed, German Jews were leaders in nearly every arena of German society: politics, law, education, science, technology, medicine, culture, and more. Absurdly, it was the Jews' high-standing in society that led to resentment among their fellow countrymen, and ultimately, their genocide.[383]

The Soviets (1917-1989)

The antisemitism of the Soviet Union, which swore it was not antisemitic but only anti-capitalist, anti-imperialist, anti-colonialist, and anti-Zionist, echoes the Nazis' racial version of antisemitism and informs a great deal of antisemitism from the political left today. As the Russian monarchy was overthrown, the incoming communists began demonizing Jews for their

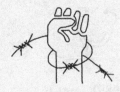

THE WARSAW GHETTO UPRISING

Contrary to the common myth that during the Holocaust, Europe's Jews were killed without much of a fight, "like sheep to the slaughter," the Jews *did fight back*. One of the most stunning examples of Jewish heroism during the Holocaust was in the ghetto in the Polish city of Warsaw, which was once one of the most Jewish cities in the world. On the eve of Passover, 1943, when the Germans entered the ghetto intending to deport the vast majority of its Jews to the extermination camps, Jewish resistance fighters ambushed them: throwing Molotov cocktails and hand grenades from alleyways, sewers, and windows. A few dozen Germans were killed in the fighting, which ended in the murder of thousands of Jews and the destruction of the ghetto. The Jews knew that the rebellion was highly unlikely to be successful, yet they refused to allow the Nazis to decide the time and place of their deaths.[384]

particular way of living. Hebrew was abolished as were Jewish religious practices and any Zionist organizations. A group of communist Jews were deputized by the state – the **Yevsektsiya** – to find Jews breaking the law and arrest them, often leading to their torture and/or execution. In the end, even the members of the Yevsektsiya came under suspicion for "anti-revolutionary" activity, and were ultimately arrested and killed as well.[385]

Later, in 1952, **Josef Stalin** became paranoid that the Jewish doctors of Russia were subverting his regime, and arrested a great many. Known as the **Doctor's Plot**, the libel accompanied a wave of propaganda against the dangers of "Zionism" in

The Soviets (1917-1989) *(cont.)*

medicine.[386] Many claim that had Stalin not died suddenly from a stroke, there would have been a mass killing of the Jews in Russia. There were even plans to deport the entire Jewish population to remote areas of Siberia.[387] In the winter of 1953, several dozen prominent Jewish journalists and artists were arrested on suspicion of "Zionist treason," even though many were vocally loyal to the Soviet Union. They were summarily shot in prison in an event known as the **Night of the Murdered Poets**.[388]

In 1975, the Soviet Union sponsored UN Resolution 3379 which proclaimed Zionism a form of racism. In her final decades, after the banning of Hebrew and attending Jewish religious services, Russia made it extremely difficult for Jews to make *aliyah* to Israel and arrested those who stood up for it, including **Natan Sharansky**, who spent nine years in a Russian prison before finally moving to Israel with fellow *refuseniks*, going on to become a celebrated Israeli politician and human rights activist.[389]

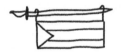

The Pan-Arabists (1945-1980)

In the wake of the fall of the Ottoman Empire, **Pan-Arabism** emerged as a secular movement for the Arabs to unify against colonial powers. Influenced a great deal by Nazi ideology, the Pan-Arabists believed in the unification of all Arabs in a singular nation-state. Pan-Arabists Gamal Abdel Nasser of Egypt and Hafez Assad of Syria considered the presence of a Jewish state in the middle of several Arab countries an insult to the pride of Arabs and Muslims so great that it justified declaring war on Israel numerous times. Indeed, during the wars of 1948 (Independence), 1967 (the Six Day War), 1973 (Yom Kippur), and in the years between, Pan-Arabist propaganda infested places like Egypt, Jordan, and Syria with a Holocaust-like viciousness, including racist stereotypes of Jews and calls for genocide. [390]

The Islamists (1970-Present)

Unlike Pan-Arabism, Islamism sought to unify the Arabs around the religion of Islam. Islamism remains popular as a political movement in the Middle East, and with it comes Islamic antisemitism. Originally, this phenomenon began with the beginning of Islam, when Jewish subjects in conquered lands were given "**dhimmi**," status as a protected second-class citizen forced to pay a special tax. But in the era of the state of Israel, Islam animates a whole list of accusations against Israel and its Jews, combining Nazi, Soviet, and Christian antisemitism with Pan-Arabist political views, accusing Jews and Israel of being an arm of Western colonialism and simultaneously demonic. Islamic antisemitism is responsible for a majority of terror attacks against Israel, and produces propaganda in every corner of the Muslim world.[391]

Left-Wing Antisemitism

Left-wing antisemitism is alive and well in America, particularly in academic institutions where it is often embedded in the curriculum of all ages, especially for college students. Its ideological mother is Soviet antisemitism, born long before the Russian Revolution with **Karl Marx**'s idea that Jewish people exploit capitalism by their very nature. On the Jewish Question, Marx once wrote, "Money is the jealous god of Israel, in the face of which no other god may exist...," an idea which rapidly spread across Europe.[399]

When the new State of Israel was born, left-wing antisemitism proliferated, but the target became "Zionism," rather than capitalism. In the 1960s and '70s, the USSR created the "Israel equals – [insert something evil here]" equation, as in "Israel equals Nazism," or "...capitalism," "...colonialism," "...imperialism," etc. This political strategy distracted the ailing Russian working class from taking issue with their own leaders. After the fall of the Soviet Union, the words describing Israel transitioned to reflect the evils of the era: "apartheid," "white supremacy," and finally, "genocide." These words don't describe Zionism or Israel, but rather the most hated things of a given society, to conflate Jews with evil and redirect anger.[400]

Contemporary left-wing antisemites often defend themselves by stating, "I was only criticizing Israel." Sociologist David Hirsh calls this mechanism the **Livingstone Formulation**, in honor of the former Mayor of London Ken Livingstone, who routinely repeated Soviet-inspired antisemitic tropes under the guise of criticizing Israel. This linguistic trick turns the conversation away from racism against Jews and towards Israeli government policy, and enables the antisemite to directly or indirectly accuse the Jews of bigotry, "silencing free speech," "being racist toward Palestinians," and so forth.[401]

Right-Wing Antisemitism

Right-wing antisemitism has been a growing source of extremism for years in America. Before World War II in the 1930s, the German-American Bund hosted a Nazi Rally in Madison Square Garden.[392] Before this, an innocent young Jewish man named **Leo Frank** was lynched by a racist mob in Georgia, which led to the founding of the **Anti-Defamation League (ADL)**.[393] A recent example of right-wing antisemitism occurred at the **Unite the Right rally** in Charlottesville, Virginia, in 2017, where participants chanted *"Jews will not replace us!,"* carried tiki torches and saluted Hitler.[394] The massacre at the **Tree of Life Synagogue** in Pittsburgh in 2018 followed soon after, when a gunman killed eleven Jewish congregants after the synagogue had hosted a pro-immigration event. Both these recent events were fueled by **Neo-Nazism,** which holds Jews as inferior to whites racially, while simultaneously believing that the Jews are plotting against Western societies by introducing migrants, known as **Replacement Theory**.[395]

The **alt-right**, a phrase coined by American Neo-Nazi Richard Spencer, provides an offshoot of right-wing antisemitism and revamps centuries-old antisemitic tropes to make them useful in the modern age. Another character worth mentioning is Nick Fuentes, a popular Holocaust-denying, Hitler-admiring podcaster.[396] Other media figures include Candace Owens, a former commentator with the conservative *Daily Wire*, who now uses her own platform to incite antisemitic tropes about Jews controlling U.S. elections, the media, and Hollywood.[397] In addition, the FBI has labeled a variety of far-right paramilitary groups a threat to national security, including the **Proud Boys** and the **Ku Klux Klan**, an organization which has terrorized Black, Latino, and Jewish Americans for the last one-hundred and fifty years.[398]

"ZIONIST" AS A BAD WORD

The antisemitic language of the far-right often mimics the language of the far-left. The comments from figures like Ku Klux Klan leader **David Duke** about the dangers that Jews pose to the world are almost indistinguishable from those espoused by anti-Israel extremists. For example, one of Duke's books is entitled *Jewish Supremacism*, where he repeatedly makes the claim that Zionists control the U.S. economy and media.[402] This isn't very different from a student at Columbia University caught on video saying, "Zionists don't deserve to live", or anti-Israel protesters in London chanting, "Zionists own the media."[403]

Holocaust Revisionism

Another feature of alt-right (and sometimes far-left) antisemitism includes Holocaust denialism, which refers to attempts to downplay or reject the historical reality of the genocide of the Jewish people. Holocaust revisionists also surmise that Jews collaborated in their own destruction for their own benefit. This lunacy occurs at the highest levels of global politics with world leaders like the Ayatollah Khomenei of the Islamic Republic of Iran overseeing a Holocaust cartoon contest mocking the worst crime in history.[404] It has also infected an American rapper Ye (Kanye West) who praised Hitler (and later went on to sell millions of albums a few months later).[405]

Palestinian Antisemitism

Sadly, thanks to generations of indoctrination funded largely by U.S. tax dollars, 93% of Palestinians in the territories of the West Bank and Gaza hold extreme anti-Jewish beliefs.[406] The ideology of Palestinian leaders, particularly of Hamas, bundles Nazi, Soviet, Pan-Arabist and Islamic antisemitism into one extreme style of Jew-hatred. Palestinian antisemitism imitates Al-Qaeda and ISIS by channeling its ideology towards violence against civilians, particularly Israeli civilians, also known as jihad. This is why after the October 7th Massacre, recordings were discovered of young men excitedly calling their parents to brag and beam about how many Jews they had killed and/or abducted.[407]

Nation of Islam

The Nation of Islam (NOI) is an African-American movement founded in the 1930s that combines Islam with Black nationalism. Influential figures within the movement include Malcolm X and Mohammed Ali. Today, the NOI is led by **Louis Farrakhan**, a proud antisemite. Farrakhan has called Jewish people "Satanic," "termites," and Judaism "a deceptive lie in order [for Jews] to further their control over government and economy." He also blames Jews for degenerate behavior portrayed in Hollywood movies. Despite their antisemitism, which includes blaming Jews for the oppression of Black Americans and homosexuality, the Nation of Islam remains woefully popular in the United States.[408]

Black Hebrew Israelites

The Black Hebrew Israelites (BHI) constitute a small but vocal American religious movement that claims that present-day African-Americans are the real descendants of the ancient Israelites. Or, in other words, that the people who claim to be Jewish in America and Israel today are imposters. BHI followers believe that Jesus himself was Black and that Black people are the chosen people. There are, of course, Black Jewish people, such as the Beta Israel from Ethiopia, but BHI is completely different. In 2022, Kyrie Irving, a player on the Brooklyn Nets basketball team, was suspended without pay for promoting an antisemitic, BHI-inspired film on Twitter. Though Irving later apologized, BHI members rallied outside the Nets stadium in Brooklyn, chanting "We are the real Jews!" The Southern Poverty Law Center and the ADL both condemn the Black Hebrew Israelites for engaging in "Holocaust denial, promotion of racial segregation, and homophobia."[409]

Conspiracy Theorists

On social media today from left to right, religious to secular, across the world and across languages, antisemitic conspiracy theories proliferate and spread at the speed of light. This blob of bad ideas accuses Jews of controlling the banks, the weather, the media, and the pornography industry. It might pontificate that Jews created COVID-19 to "neuter the world's Muslim population," or that Jews were behind 9/11, and more. Despite no logic behind these theories, they still find ardent supporters. Unfortunately, this has led to more than a few antisemitic attacks in person against Jewish communities including the Colleyville hostage attack in 2022 in which an armed man, who believed Jews had immense powers, walked into a synagogue and demanded the rabbi call senior government officials in order to release a convicted Al Qaeda terrorist.[410] Oftentimes, social media users will use the terms Zionism, Israel, and Jews interchangeably in a derogatory way – another modern manifestation of antisemitism.[411]

AIPAC

The American Israel Public Affairs Committee (AIPAC) is an American bipartisan 501(c)(4) lobbying group that focuses on advancing the mutually beneficial U.S.-Israel relationship. Unfortunately, AIPAC is demonized as a nefarious "Israel lobby" and accused of "disproportionately" impacting American elections. This is false. AIPAC is strictly monitored, forbidden from acting in the interest of any foreign government, and promotes the same policies whether the Israeli government is left or right in nature. The primary legislation they advocate for is the U.S.-Israel aid package, which requires more than 80% of the aid package to be reinvested in the U.S. economy, creating U.S. jobs and spurring U.S. innovation. This is in contrast with lobbying organizations like **J Street**, which lobby the United States to pressure Israel, a sovereign country, to carry out a specific policy. Both organizations however, are completely legal and follow existing American laws when it comes to the democratic process.[412]

INTERNATIONAL HOLOCAUST REMEMBRANCE ALLIANCE

The enormity of the Holocaust required giving antisemitism a definition on the global stage. In the early 2000s, dozens of leaders and academics in the Jewish community gathered together to create the **International Holocaust Remembrance Alliance (IHRA) Working Definition of Antisemitism**. Big corporations and more than 30 countries have adopted the IHRA definition, including the European Union, and non-profit organizations use it to identify legitimately antisemitic behavior and speech. The working definition is as follows:

> *Antisemitism is a certain perception of Jews, which may be expressed as hatred toward Jews. Rhetorical and physical manifestations of antisemitism are directed toward Jewish or non-Jewish individuals and/or their property, toward Jewish community institutions and religious facilities.*

The IHRA definition does not dictate or suggest ramifications for antisemitic speech or behaviors, in contradiction to left-wing Israel activists who often accuse the definition of chilling free speech or being too punitive. The IHRA definition spells out classical antisemitic tropes, along with modern accusations against the Jewish people, such as the claim that Zionism is a racist endeavor.[413]

COMMON LIES ABOUT ISRAEL

Here are some lies about Israel that you'll hear from the people and movements that we mentioned above.

1. **LIE: "I'm Anti-Zionist, not antisemitic."**
    The vast majority of Jews around the world are Zionists or identify with Zionism. Claiming a problem with the liberation movement and self-determination of an entire minority group is inherently antisemitic, regardless of intent. During the student protests against Israel in 2024, multiple administrations implied that the students setting up illegal encampments were only objecting to Israeli policy and not peddling in antisemitic tropes. In response to this, 540 Jewish students at Columbia wrote a letter stating the obvious:

    > We proudly believe in the Jewish People's right to self-determination in our historic homeland as a fundamental tenet of our Jewish identity. Contrary to what many have tried to sell you – no, Judaism cannot be separated from Israel. Zionism is, simply put, the manifestation of that belief.[414]

2. **LIE: "Israelis/Jews are white."**
    Considering that the majority of the Jews in America are of Ashkenazi descent, many in the West believe that Jews as an entire people are white. This notion feeds into the misconception that Jews are among the oppressors in regard to Western racial relations. In reality, millions

2. LIE: "Israelis/Jews are white." *(cont.)*

of Jews around the world and the majority in Israel do not have light skin and would be considered, in Western terminology, as people of color. This colorist prism through which Americans judge people by melanin affects their view of many geopolitical issues around the world. Additionally, the Jews who do look "white" are not considered white by White Supremacists. Indeed, 6 million mostly Ashkenazi Jews were killed for the very crime of not being white by Nazi Germany.

3. LIE: "Antisemitism isn't as important/prevalent as other racisms."

According to the FBI, Jews have been the most targeted religious minority in the United States for decades, more than double the number of attacks on any other religious minority.[415] Since the October 7th Massacre, this number has increased tenfold around the world.[416]

4. LIE: "Israel is a colonial state."

Colonialism is defined as a movement of foreign nationals exploiting a land for which they have no legitimate connection in service to a mother country.[417] In stark contrast, the Jewish people waited out multiple empires including Roman, Islamic, Ottoman and British before returning to their ancient Land of Israel. Their return was not in service to any other people but their own. Jews are not foreigners in the land.

DARVO

Deny Attack Reverse Victim Offender (DARVO) stands for the gas-lighting technique used against the Jewish people and the state of Israel. It works by accusing the victim of being guilty of the same crime done to him. For example, while the Jews suffered the most massive well-documented genocide at the hands of the Germans, they are relentlessly and regularly accused of this very crime, whether in the International Criminal Court or on a college campuses. Jews are also commonly called "Nazis," some of whom are descendants of Holocaust survivors. Both hurtful and outrageous, the technique is often effective at blurring the lines between who is right and who is wrong.[419]

5. **LIE: "Israel is an apartheid state."**

Apartheid is a state-enforced policy of racial segregation, one for the dominant group and another for the oppressed group. In Apartheid South Africa, buses and public spaces were divided by race, and there were specific zones throughout the country where only Black South Africans could live.[418] In Israel, people of different faiths, backgrounds, and ethnicities have equal rights under the law. Over 2 million Israelis are not Jewish, but are of Arab descent, and are highly represented in politics, law, medicine, education, technology, and entertainment (see: *Chapter 4: The Apartheid Lie*).

6. **LIE: "Israel is commiting genocide"**

The word "genocide" was coined in 1944 to refer to the mass extermination of the Jews and implies a systematic, intentional destruction of an entire people, often with a racial or religious motivation. Whenever Israel defends itself, the Jewish state is accused of committing this very crime - a vicious libel, a perfect example of DARVO. In fact, wars are rarely symmetrical or "proportional." For example, approximately three thousand Americans were killed on 9/11, but hundreds of thousands of Iraqis and Afghans were killed in the resultant wars. Around twenty four hundred American soldiers were killed in the Japanese attack on Pearl Harbor, but no one accused the U.S. of genocide when they dropped two atomic bombs wiping out the populations of entire cities. Contrary to this accusation, the Palestinian population in the West Bank and Gaza has increased steadily over the last several decades, according to official Palestinian statistics.[420]

LIE: "Jews and Arabs lived in peace before 1948."

7. While Jews and Arabs did live in what is now Israel for hundreds of years together, there were always attacks on Jewish communities in the territory. One such example is the Hebron Massacre in 1929 where Arabs massacred Jews in the cities of Safed and Hebron. In 1936, because Arabs did not want Jews fleeing the Holocaust to settle in Britain's Mandate for Palestine, violence against Jewish communities erupted in what is known as the **Great Arab Revolt**, which resulted in 547 murdered Jews in pre-state Israel.[421] For a full list of pogroms by Arabs against Jews, see 10ThingsEveryJewShouldKnow.com/pogroms.

8. **LIE: "There would be a Palestinian state if Israel agreed."**
    Palestinians have been offered some form of a state multiple times (see: *Chapter 4: Palestinian Statehood Rejectionism*). At any point during the Egyptian control of Gaza or Jordanian control of the West Bank, Palestinians could have declared a state but did not. Why have they rejected it? Because, among other things, Palestinian leadership is financially incentivized to always reject a state, and the Palestinian people's foundational ethos is the rejection of a Jewish state in any borders, even if this means they remain totally without a state of their own.

9. **LIE: "The IDF uses disproportionate force."**
    International law acknowledges that "proportionality" carried out by states in warfare is necessary for a military objective. Casualty discrepancies between Israelis and Palestinians are two-fold. Firstly, they result from Israeli society treasuring human life and investing in defensive technology such as the Iron Dome and bomb shelters for every citizen whereas Palestinians and their children are celebrated for becoming martyrs. In Gaza, all underground tunnels which could have been used as shelters for civilians are instead used to protect Hamas leaders and weapons. Secondly, casualty reports are used as a method of information warfare wherein Palestinian deaths are exaggerated or reported before it is possible to know or conduct an investigation.[422]

LIE: "The IDF uses disproportionate force." *(cont.)*

Every civilian casualty is tragic. In general, the proportion of the civilian casualties between Israel and Palestinians is markedly less than other conflicts. Hundreds of thousands of civilians were killed by Americans after the attacks of Pearl Harbor and 9/11 in response to proportionally a small amount of deaths. The global average civilian to combatant ratio is 9 civilians killed for every 1 combatant. The IDF's rate is far less. In an Israeli 2023 operation in Jenin in the West Bank, the civilian to combatant ratio was .6 Palestinian civilians for every one terrorist killed – almost unheard of even in modern warfare.[423]

ANTISEMITIC CHANTS AND WHAT THEY MEAN

There is only one solution, intifada, revolution.
The aim of an intifada is the killing of Israelis and complete elimination of the Jewish state. It does not express defense or support of Palestinian rights.

Resistance is justified when people are occupied.
This chant expresses support for armed violence against Jews and Israelis in the same language as that used by terrorist organizations like Hamas and Islamic Jihad.

Globalize the intifada.

Intifada is an Arabic word that means "uprising" but has only ever been used to refer to violent riots and waves of terror attacks. In the Second Intifada in Israel, thousands of Israelis and Palestinians were killed. The concept of "globalizing" such an event is a call to murder Jews and foment violence everywhere they reside. As Jewish novelist **Dara Horn** notes, "Intifada means uprising just like Sieg Hiel (the Nazi salute) meant only 'hail victory.'"[425]

We don't want two states, we want all of it.

This is a rejection of the right of Israel to exist in any borders.

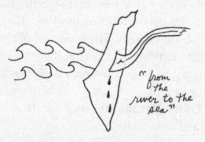

From the river to the sea, Palestine will be free.

This is an anglicized version of the Arabic chant which translates to, "From the water to the water, Palestine is Arab," which calls for the ethnic cleansing of Jews from the region.[424] The popularized version in the West falsely portrays Palestinians as the only people indigenous to the land. It calls for the complete elimination of the State of Israel and can mean the genocide of Jews living within the land.

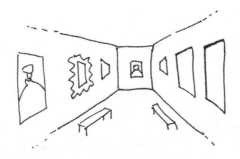

MISINFORMATION HALL OF FAME

BDS: Boycott, Divestment, and Sanctions

The **Boycott, Divestment, and Sanctions (BDS)** movement seeks to destroy Israel by preventing it from participating in the global economy and encouraging all entities to avoid doing business with the state. While the BDS movement originated on university campuses in the name of social justice, it has spread to other areas as well, such as corporation boardrooms and city halls. Its explicitly stated goals are to dismantle the Jewish state of Israel, not end the occupation of the West Bank, or to cease the construction of settlements. The reality of BDS is that it hurts Palestinians. Until the recent Gaza war, there were over 100,000 Palestinians working in Israel on a near daily basis.[426] Ironically, The Boycott, Divestment, and Sanctions Movement (BDS) was co-founded by **Omar Barghouti**, an Arab Israeli citizen who studied at an Israeli university.[427]

Democratic Socialists of America

Members of the **Democratic Socialists of America (DSA)**, a far left offshoot of the Democratic Party, have repeatedly spread libelous claims about Israel and Zionism on social media, contributing to the escalation in antisemitic commentary online. On October 8th, 2023, a day after the October 7th Massacre, the DSA held a demonstration "to fight for the liberation of Palestine."[428] DSA-endorsed members of Congress include Rashida Tlaib (D-MI), Ilhan Omar (D-MN), and (until recently) Alexandria Ocasio-Cortez (D-NY).

Students for Justice in Palestine/Within Our Lifetime
Campus hate groups such as **Students for Justice in Palestine (SJP)** and **Within Our Lifetime (WOL)** play a huge role in contributing to the rise in antisemitism and harassment of Jewish students on U.S. campuses. They support terrorist activities by Hamas and PFLP and advocate for BDS. These groups do not advocate for a two state solution or any peaceful resolution to the Israeli-Palestinian conflict, but rather "resistance by any means necessary" in the region. SJP's definition of "justice" is *undoing* the fundamental injustice of Israel's establishment. They have been banned from multiple campuses for their harassment and calls to violence especially since October 7th, and have even recently resorted to shutting down American airports, streets, and bridges with their demonstrations.[429]

Jewish Voice for Peace/If Not Now
Jewish Voice for Peace (JVP) and If Not Now (INN) are anti-Zionist organizations who claim to stand for Jewish values and oppose the existence of the State of Israel on moral grounds. In practice, these groups are not representative of the Jewish community, and engage in antisemitic rhetoric and harassment, including support for terrorism and calling for "intifada." Both INN and JVP have even held vigils for Palestinians who have murdered Jews who were subsequently eliminated by the IDF. Their presence at rallies or in the signatories of letters condemning Israel provide cover in the face of accusations of antisemitism.[430]

HIJACKED CAUSES

Anti-Israel agitators have been known to hijack causes that have nothing to do with Israel in order to spread their messaging, often with the ultimatum that, unless progressives join the cause to eradicate Israel, they are not true progressives. This radicalizes other groups organized around a domestic issue into supporting terror organizations abroad, and effectively pushes Jews from social justice spaces, where many of them are used to feeling welcomed.

Black Lives Matter

The recent antisemitism in America has driven a wedge between what was once a great and important partnership between the Jewish and Black communities. A group of Jews along with African-American activists founded the National Association for the Advancement of Colored People (NAACP) and also played a significant role in the Civil Rights Movement of the 1960s.[431] Bafflingly, many chapters of the contemporary organization, **Black Lives Matter**, have adopted an explicit anti-Zionist position in their platform. For example, after the October 7th Massacre, BLM Chicago posted a photo of a terrorist on a paraglider on their Instagram pages in solidarity with Hamas. It is important to remember that Black Americans are not a monolith, and many reject what the movement stands for, including its hatred of Israel.[432]

Feminism

After the October 7th Massacre in Israel, the world reacted with a surge in rape and sexual assault denial, despite confessions from Hamas terrorists who committed the massacres that they abused and raped Israeli women. Many Western feminist organizations, including *UN Women*, were silent for months.[433] In feminist circles, excluding Jewish women from activism has become common. The 2017 **Women's March** in the United States, which organized millions of women to protest in Washington, D.C., at the prospect of the Trump Administration's potential assault on women's reproductive rights and social freedoms, came under pressure when several of its leaders, including Palestinian-American activist Linda Sarsour, praised antisemitic leader Louis Farrakhan and called feminism and Zionism "incompatible." Tamika Mallory, another leader of the Women's March, openly supports Louis Farrakhan and has accused Jews of "upholding white supremacy."[434]

LGBT Equality

Certain groups of LGBT people connect themselves to anti-Zionist causes. This is striking considering how homosexuality is considered a sin in mainstream Palestinian culture. Many who identify as gay have even been executed by authorities.[435] In this case, agitators take advantage of "useful idiots" who know little on the subject by using language like "justice," "freedom," and "liberation" to tether two causes together that have nothing to do with one another. Anti-Israel activists will often accuse LGBT Jewish people who have a strong connection with Israel of **pink-washing**, that is, talking about how safe it is to be LGBT in Israel to avoid talking about the Palestinians. In reality, the accusation of pink-washing is usually a mechanism to make LGBT Jews and Israelis feel uncomfortable in LGBT, usually progressive, spaces. [436]

Climate Change

Sadly, even the cause of climate change has been captured ideologically. Famed Swedish environmentalist Greta Thunberg now dawns a keffiyeh and chants, "intifada, revolution," at rallies to ban fossil fuels.[437] At the UN's Climate Change Conference in Europe, protestors held signs reading, "Palestine is a climate change issue."[438] In 2021, the Sunrise Movement, perhaps the most popular climate action movement in the U.S. especially among young people, refused to participate in a rally in Washington, D.C., in support of D.C. statehood and expanded voting rights, because a variety of Jewish (non-Israel related) organizations were also participating.[439] In reality, Palestinian society is no champion of environmental protection. One of the primary tactics of Gaza terrorists in 2018 was launching airborne arson attacks using kites to destroy countless fields and agricultural farms in southern Israel.[440]

HUMAN
RIGHTS
WATCH

Human Rights Watch

Human Rights Watch (HRW), founded in 1978 by Jewish publishing CEO Robert Bernstein, began with the noble mission of confronting human rights abuses by totalitarian regimes around the world, particularly, in the Soviet Union. But in 1993, Kenneth Roth stepped in as Executive Director, and the organization's values changed. Instead of going after leaders actively violating human rights, Roth's HRW undertook an anti–western agenda: criticizing democracies rather than dictatorships. HRW played a prominent role in the antisemitic hate fest that commenced in Durban, South Africa in 2001 at the UN Conference Against Racism (See: Chapter 6). After continued and obsessive condemnation of Israel under Roth, in 2009, Bernstein publicly denounced the organization he had created. The organization continued to hire staff members vocally supportive of a boycott against Israel, and in 2021, falsely accused Israel of being an apartheid state with an academic report filled with pseudo-research and propaganda. After the October 7th massacre, HRW began harshly condemning Israel's military action in Gaza while underplaying Hamas's assault, leading Danielle Haas, an HRW senior editor, to publicly resign over the organization's "shattered professionalism, abandoned principles of accuracy and fairness." The HRW has come under fire for accepting large donations from authoritarian regimes in the Middle East including Saudi Arabia and Libya.[441] While founded by a Jew, in the recent past it has followed in the path of the UN in issuing distorted and false statistics to malign Israel around the world.

Amnesty International

Amnesty International began as a London-based human rights organization with the intention of advancing freedoms all around the world. Yet, also like HRW, Amnesty exhibited a glaring anti-Israel bias. In 2022, Amnesty released its own report accusing Israel of practicing apartheid, claiming that Israeli Arabs are subjected to a different legal system than Israeli Jews, which is false, and also failed to condemn Palestinian and Arab violence against Israel, whitewashing the military predicament Israel faces at all times. In the wake of the October 7th Massacre, Amnesty has repeatedly accused Israel of bringing violence upon itself while ignoring the actions of Palestinians. From October 7 to October 30, Amnesty International's main account posted 23 times about the war: 13 posts exclusively focused on Gazan suffering and allegations of Israeli violations, and five called for a ceasefire and only 2 mentioned Israeli hostages. Amnesty falsely accuses Israel of genocide and regularly calls for a total arms embargo.[442]

The International Criminal Court
The **International Criminal Court (ICC)** was established in 2002 by way of the Rome Statute, an international treaty that spells out which crimes the court can investigate and produce rulings on: war crimes, crimes against humanity, genocide, and aggression. The ICC is meant to step in when a state's judicial system cannot independently judge crimes taking place within their borders. Neither Israel nor the United States are members or signatories of the statute, which includes many hostile and anti-democratic regimes who regularly accuse Israel of crimes to distract from their own human rights violations. The ICC has no jurisdiction to prosecute Israelis, considering Israel is not a "Member State" and has its own independent judicial system. In 2024, the ICC issued arrest warrants for Prime Minister Benjamin Netanyahu and Defense Minister Yoav Gallant for war crimes in Gaza, the first ruling against a democratic country in its history. The ICC had no arrest warrants against Kim Jong-il in North Korea, nor Bashar Al Assad in Syria, a notorious war criminal.[443]

DEI: "Diversity, Equity, and Inclusion"
After the death of George Floyd in Minneapolis, America boiled over with rage against police brutality and racism in the United States. Diversity, Equity, and Inclusion (DEI), while established decades earlier, became popular among organizations in order to address systematic oppression by way of proposing that all oppressed groups share a struggle and only by "leveling the playing field" can justice be achieved. People's level of oppression can be based on skin color, sex and sexual orientation, among other things, says DEI. In this scenario, white heterosexual males constitute the most privileged de facto oppressor class. Since some Western-assimilated Jews (often Ashkenazi) have light skin and may be perceived as white, and

Israelis are libeled as "colonizers," Jews may be seen in this context as oppressors despite being historically and consistently oppressed for millennia.[444] Also – Jews, like any other group, have diverse backgrounds, colors, and experiences, and do not fit easily into any constructed binaries of race or ethnicity.

WHY THE JEWS?

People use the Jews as scapegoats because, prior to Israel, the Jews couldn't fight back and had nowhere to go – Jews had few rights, nor land, army, nor political power of their own. There was nothing an antisemite had to lose when letting off a little steam by burning down a synagogue. However, in the post-Holocaust age, the Jewish people do have a land, an army, and political power of their own. Jews should take pride in who they are and work to understand why the Jewish people have outlasted every civilization that sought to destroy them.

8

THE MEDIA

There are always two wars occurring in any given conflict. One is on the battlefield with soldiers, guns, rockets, and helmets. The other is through the eyes and the minds of the public, called "the narrative." In our new age of media and social media (which has only been around since the early 2000s), this battlefield is intense, sometimes dangerous, and fraught with constantly shifting misinformation. Despite it not involving actual blood, it is important to understand the terrain. The media regularly presents the Israeli-Palestinian conflict as if Israel is the superpower and the Palestinians are, without question, the underdog. The reality is that Jews are a miniscule percentage of the population, and Israel is an even smaller country surrounded by twenty-two Arab nations. Jews, despite the conspiracy theories of both the right and left, do not control the media; to the contrary, they're vastly outnumbered.

To make matters more complex, every demographic has a different means of getting information. Older populations get news from TV and newspaper outlets, both their paper and online version, whereas younger people get their news almost exclusively online via social media apps. This divide has led to a deterioration in the quality and depth of research and reporting. Unfortunately, too many people are either not familiar with or don't believe in media bias whether from the mainstream or on social media.[445] Impressive numbers of followers on social media can be faked, exaggerated, or artificially inflated. And even if it is authentically popular, that doesn't make it correct.

Because the audience of this book is young people, let's start with a young person's primary means of receiving news: social media.

SOCIAL MEDIA

For the first time in history, information can be disseminated to millions of people in a matter of seconds, creating an environment where disinformation can spread just as quickly without any verification. As the famous adage goes: "A lie makes its way halfway around the world while the truth is putting on its shoes." One can write a well-researched post, with citations, multiple points of view, and historical context, and no one will see it if others don't interact with it. Social media increases radicalization and political polarization. Clicks and likes encourage outrageous headlines, claims, and ideas about people and world events, with little to no regulation.

Each social media platform has its strengths and weaknesses when it comes to addressing incendiary speech and disinformation. Here's the basic run-down for each of the most known platforms today. It's important to note that in other countries, there are other platforms that are far more popular. For example in China, *WeChat* is used, in Russia, *Vkontakte*, and in Japan, *Line*, all a bit different from our apps.

X, formerly known as Twitter

X is a fast-paced platform with text, video, and photo functionality that can both facilitate and hinder meaningful discourse, owned by **Elon Musk**. While X faces criticism for its response to hate speech and harassment under the management of Elon Musk,[446] some wonder if the October 7th attacks would have been characterized differently were it not for the unfettered access to images of the massacre on X versus other outlets. The flipside of this free speech policy is that it also allows even terrorist financiers like the Supreme Leader of Islamic Republic, Ayatollah Khomenei, to post statements like, "...The Zionists suck the blood of a country for their own benefit when they gain a foothold in a country. Those helping the Zionist Regime are helping bring their own destruction."[447]

Facebook

As one of the largest social media platforms, Facebook (owned by Meta) employs algorithms that favor posts which elicit a reaction (particularly if it is a negative one.)[448] It grapples with issues related to misinformation and hate speech. It has implemented policies to combat hate, but enforcement can be inconsistent. The demographic on Facebook skews significantly older than other social media platforms, and content that is apolitical is favored by the algorithm.

Instagram

Owned by Meta, Instagram is a visual platform where imagery plays a significant role. It's one of the most popular platforms, especially for a younger demographic, but today faces significant challenges in properly responding with incitement to violence, antisemitism, and targeted harassment.[449] A report from 2021 found millions of results for hashtags relating to antisemitic conspiracy theories – including "#gasjews" and #Hitlerwasright.[450] While October 7th made the app markedly more political, any individual should think of it more like a business card for future employers where people will make snap judgements and first impressions by looking at your profile. Posting political content, unless it is ephemeral, is not advised unless your goal is to become a political activist.

YouTube

YouTube, owned by Google, is the hub for video content, primarily long-form, but with the establishment of YouTube "shorts," that may be changing. While the platform offers opportunities for education and advocacy, it also faces challenges related to the spread of radical politics, particularly right-wing extremism. Google monitors hate speech and incitements to violence more rigorously than other platforms,[451] yet still, after the October 7th Massacre, there was a fifty-one fold surge in antisemitic comments on Youtube, including dehumanizing comments and conspiracy theories about Jewish power.[452]

TikTok

This rapidly growing platform has faced scrutiny for its handling of hate speech and harmful content, especially considering it is the most popular platform amongst teens and young adults. A study conducted between February 2020 to May 2021 by Weimann and Masri found on Tik Tok a 41% increase in antisemitic posts, a 912% increase in antisemitic comments and a 1,375% increase in antisemitic usernames.[453] Since October 7th, the problem has grown worse. A recent study found that spending just thirty minutes on TikTok a day increased the chances of holding antisemitic or anti-Israel views by 17%.[454] In 2023, Jewish American celebrities signed a letter to TikTok stating the app was not safe for Jewish users.[455]

TikTok has also faced criticism for blatant political bias and censorship.[456] TikTok is owned by ByteDance, a Chinese company, and has been harshly criticized by U.S. lawmakers for its affiliation with the **Chinese Communist Party (CCP)**. U.S. government employees are not allowed to have TikTok on their phone, and the U.S. Congress recently passed a bill requiring TikTok's parent company, ByteDance, to sell to an owner that is not an "adversarial country," or else be banned in the United States.[457] The purpose of this bill, which was passed with broad bipartisan support, is to stop the involvement of the CCP in the platform.

Telegram and Whatsapp

Both Telegram and WhatsApp have rolled out channels allowing users to publish running updates at all times, similar to a newsfeed on Facebook or X. These new forums have been particularly popular with alt-right and neo-Nazi groups who have been kicked off of other platforms. The ADL reports that after the October 7th Massacre, there was a 433.76% increase in violent antisemitic posts on Telegram, jumping from an average of 283.12 points a day to 1271 posts. Post October 7th, the number of antisemitic posts has not returned to previous levels.[458]

UNDERSTANDING ALGORITHMS

If you know anything about social media, you've probably heard the term **algorithm** before. How do they work? Algorithms are a formula that decides what you see based on what you've watched and liked. If you like a picture with cats playing, you will be shown more videos of cats playing, and possibly other animals, in the hopes of keeping your attention on the app longer. Large companies create algorithms that manipulate what you see in order to maximize your engagement and time spent on their particular app. Inherently, this makes social media ripe for extremism.[459]

CENSORSHIP

Censorship of Jewish, pro-Israel voices is chronic on all the platforms. On TikTok, studies have proven the censorship of certain political views and the artificial inflation of opposing views on conflicts such as Israel-Palestine (elevating the Palestinian position), India-Kashmir (elevating the Kashmir position), China-Taiwan (elevating the Chinese position), and Russia-Ukraine (elevating Russia's position).[460] Other platforms also face challenges. On Instagram, the Islamic Republic of Iran has been accused of bribing content moderators to remove content critical of the regime.[461] Meta has also faced criticism over the removal and censorship of pro-Israel voices as well as their failure to remove incitement to terrorism on the Palestinian side.[462] This is an ongoing challenge that numerous stakeholders and NGOs regularly meet with social media companies to address, but no solution has been put forward.

Bullying

Since Israel's 2021 Guardian of the Walls operation in Gaza, social media has become a breeding ground for antisemitic harassment. Simple Jewish holiday greetings from politicians, sports clubs, or corporations are bombarded with comments attacking Israel and "Zionism," sometimes so severe and violent in nature that accounts are forced to take a "Happy Passover" post down. This has had a chilling effect on free speech. Allies think twice before voicing any kind of support for anything related to the Jewish people. In 2021, after Israel's Guardian of the Walls operation in Gaza, three young German Jews told researchers that being on the receiving end of antisemitism on social media led to a "loss of control," "unawareness as to what would happen next," and despair over "the silence of others."[463]

Disinformation

Deliberate false information, aka propaganda, plays a huge role in shaping public opinion. (Note: *misinformation* implies incorrect information that is unintentionally misleading; whereas *disinformation* is designed to mislead on purpose). Disinformation spreads like wildfire on social media and has led to a variety of tragedies, including the shooting at the Pittsburgh Tree of Life Synagogue in 2018 (the shooter had been shown "evidence" on social media of Jews planning to "replace" the white population in America with immigrants).[464]

Disinformation on social media works hard to falsely portray Israel as the most oppressive nation in the world and Jews who support Israel as racist, violent individuals. Influencer campaigns accelerate the spread of disinformation on social media and alter public opinion. When people like Bella Hadid, who often spreads antisemitic libels against Jews and Israel, have over 60 million followers, four times the amount of Jews in the entire world, it is clearly an unfair fight. Further, many nations, including China, Turkey, Iran, and Russia, use bots – unverified accounts that are created using a computer program but made to look like actual people. Often, tens of thousands of bots are unleashed to parrot phrases and views to foment a desired narrative.[465]

U.S. TELEVISION/LEGACY MEDIA

U.S. television news stations tend to offer a shallow analysis of world events, without adequate context or balanced coverage of why what's happening is happening. Here are how some of the U.S. networks have fared in their reporting of the Israeli-Palestinian conflict.

CNN

During the 2021 war between Gaza and Israel, when Gaza fired over 30,000 rockets at Israel, the top of the news on **CNN** always opened with Israel's response, misleading audiences into thinking that Israel's defensive measures were unprovoked.[466] In the 2023-24 Gaza War, initially CNN would cite exaggerated casualty reports from the **Gaza Ministry of Health** but later amended their reporting to note that these numbers do not differentiate between civilians and combatants.[467] CNN has also gone to lengths to amplify the stories of kidnapped Israeli hostages, allowing Americans and others in the West to grasp the full scope of the tragedy.

TERROR ORGANIZATIONS AS SOURCES

Democratic countries prize freedom of speech and expression.
This unfortunately opens a window for nefarious actors to peddle
in distorted facts and figures to create a strategic narrative. News
organizations in both democratic and non-democratic nations
participate in all manner of distortions. In authoritarian countries like
Russia and Iran, only one narrative is allowed to break through to
the public, representing only one agenda. Since terror organizations
and other guerilla, non-state actors often lie about what happens on
the ground in an area where they are fighting, media outlets rarely
rely on their reporting. The only time the media relies on terrorist
organizations' reporting is when Israel is actively fighting its enemies.
The international media would never consider ISIS a reliable source
for casualty rates in the city of Mosul, but it often accepts and repeats
reports and data published by the terrorist organization of Hamas
without asking questions.[468] This resulted in countless instances since
October 7th that major news networks referred to the Gaza Ministry of
Health (i.e: Hamas) for casualty numbers that were later revised to be
much lower.

MSNBC

MSNBC exhibits a clear anti-Israel bias in most of its reporting. The network's phraseology often relays a narrative that the conflict is, "Israel versus the Palestinians," rather than, "Israel against Hamas." Clickbait headlines designed to attract reader attention include, "Israel kills x number of Palestinians in airstrike," lacking differentiation between Hamas militants and Palestinian civilians.[469] In 2023, after the October 7th Massacre, CEO of the Anti-Defamation League, Jonathan Greenblatt, appeared on the popular MSNBC program, *Morning Joe* where he sharply criticized the network's coverage of the brutal terrorist attack saying:

> *Please stop calling this a retaliation. This is a defensive measure against an organization that is committed to one thing: killing Jews. Not a peaceful resolution of a conflict, but murdering Jews. And if you're wondering if I'm exaggerating, please, I beg of you, everyone watching and everyone at this network, just watch the footage.*[470]

Some of MSNBC's news anchors and journalists have problematic records on the Israeli-Palestinian conflict. Mehdi Hassan (now removed from the network) was accused of exhibiting anti-Israel bias and his demotion which led to him quitting was not explained. Another MSNBC political commentator, Ayman Mohyeldin, falsely claimed during a live broadcast in Jerusalem that a Palestinian terrorist who had committed a stabbing attack was unarmed, while the network simultaneously showed a photo of the assailant holding a knife. Joy Reid, with her own show, *The ReidOut*, has posted on social media unverified information about Israel's war against Hamas on numerous occasions.[471]

Fox

Fox News has been one of the more fair networks when it comes to the Israel-Gaza war in 2023, but the network is also known for having a right-wing bias and making the conflict an American partisan issue, which it is not. Fox is less likely to take data and sources from terrorist organizations such as the Gaza Health Ministry numbers in the midst of war at face value. Many of their commentators are outwardly protective of America's most important ally in the Middle East and more pro-Israel in general.

INTERNATIONAL MEDIA

International networks reporting on the Israeli-Palestinian conflict all follow similar patterns: Israeli claims are met with skepticism, and at times the Israeli narrative isn't represented at all, whereas the claims of the Palestinians are taken as absolute fact, often without any verification or comment from the Israeli side. Israel is often blamed for all that ails the Palestinians including violence within Palestinian society, whereas Palestinians, even terrorists, are portrayed as acting "in response" to vague, unproven accusations of oppression by Israel. AP, Reuters, Sky News, and other international networks have significantly more reporters based in Israel than in any other even more dangerous locations at any given time, simply because Israel is known to robustly protect freedom of the press.[472] Being a beacon of freedom in the Middle East means that international networks disproportionately focus their coverage on Israel, because there are no negative consequences for their criticisms. The same cannot be said for undemocratic countries, making it so that Israel is often subjected to a disproportionate amount of attention.

PALLYWOOD

Pallywood refers to the use of fake, staged, or altered photos and videos of what's happening in the Israel-Palestine region, especially during wartime. In every IDF operation since 2005, the Internet becomes drenched with photos and videos depicting inhumane cruelty being carried out against Palestinians, usually children. The perpetrator's goal is to make the content go viral, and only upon further inspection is the reporting discovered to be fake or staged. Pictures of children in hospitals that are said to be Palestinian are sometimes later revealed to be from the Syrian Civil War.[473] AI generated photos[474] of civilians designed to elicit strong emotional reactions online proliferate unabated.

Other examples of Pallywood include narrative meddling, such as when, in 2018, eight-month-old infant Layla Ghandour died due to a rare blood disease that ran in her family. At the time of her death, however, Palestinians were violently rioting against Israel at the Gaza border. The media reported that **Layla Ghandour** had died as a result of Israeli tear gas being fired on innocent Gazans. The story of the baby's purported death at the hands of Israel dominated global media at the time. A later investigation revealed that Hamas's Yahya Sinwar had actually *paid* the Ghandour family to tell the media that the child was killed at the protest against Israel, despite dying from illness. Ghandour's picture is still today circulated around social media as a weapon of libel against Jews and Israelis.[475]

STATE-SPONSORED MEDIA

State-sponsored media outlets, heavily influenced and funded by the government of a given country, need to be taken into consideration when analyzing coverage of global events, in order to discern whose narrative is being propagated.

The Al Jazeera Network

Founded in Qatar and receiving an enormous sum of money from the Qatari government,[476] **Al Jazeera**'s coverage is different inside and outside the Middle East. Inside, the network foments Islamist propaganda and routinely traffics in antisemitic tropes and justifications of terrorism that harm all people, Muslims included. For example, Al Jazeera has produced content claiming that the number of Jews who were killed in the Holocaust had been exaggerated by the Zionist movement, and that Israel was "the biggest winner" from it.[477] During the Second Intifada, Palestinians who had been killed were referred to as "martyrs" by the network, a word meaning one who dies valiantly for a political cause. The newsroom threw an on-air birthday party for Hezbollah terrorist Samir Kuntar in 2008, who murdered an Israeli child with the butt of his rifle.[478] Many claim that Al Jazeera is linked financially to the Muslim Brotherhood.[479] In English, the network often broadcasts and creates progressive left-wing content, even pro-LGBT and feminist content giving liberals a false signal to trust their content as it relates to Israel and the Palestine Territories. Although Al-Jazeera had maintained a bureau in Jerusalem since the early 2000s, their questionable reporting and accused collaboration with terrorist groups like Hamas led Israel to close its operations in 2024.[480] Al Jazeera is currently banned in Saudi Arabia, Bahrain, U.A.E., Jordan, Iraq, Egypt, Sudan, Israel, Yemen and most recently the Palestinian Authority in the West Bank.

AL JAZEERA'S HAMAS CRIME BLINDNESS

Al Jazeera's Gaza coverage actively avoids Hamas' crimes against Palestinians, notably, abruptly cutting off[481] one interview in Gaza when a Palestinian began to criticize Hamas. Like American outlets, Al Jaeera repeatedly cites Hamas's casualty numbers as fact. Al Jazeera also reported in August 2024[482] that a poll was conducted in Israel showing that 47% of Israelis believe Palestinian terrorist detainees should be raped. No such poll took place, and the original source was a photoshopped graphic on social media.It was also discovered that some of Al Jazeera's journalists in the Gaza area, working as freelance correspondents or photographers, had ties to Hamas, and some were even at the scene of the October 7th Massacre. Two of their correspondents, Ismail Abu Omar and Mohammed Washah, have been confirmed to be Hamas commanders.[483] In October of 2024, the IDF released documents that proved six additional members of the Al Jazeera press team were Hamas militants, including snipers, rocket-launchers, and battalion commanders.[484] Al Jazeera further claimed that images released of murdered Israeli babies on October 7th by Hamas were AI-generated. Independent analysts found that Al Jazeera had themselves used AI generated photos to deceive their audience about the events of October 7th.[485]

BBC

The British Broadcasting Company (BBC) is the government-sponsored media of the United Kingdom. In 2024, British researchers discovered that in the course of its reporting on the Israel-Hamas war, the BBC violated its editorial guidelines more than 1,500 times, "showing a distinct pattern of bias against Israel." According to the data, the BBC mentioned Israel as "committing war crimes" four times more than Hamas (127 versus 30,) fourteen times more as "committing genocide," (283 versus 19,) and six times more as violating international law (167 versus 27.)[486] Additionally, the network has suffered repeated scandals concerning antisemitic reporters and staff members. BBC dismissed presenter Tala Halawa for tweeting "Hitler was right," but only after social media pressure.[487] In February 2024, BBC's Dawn Queva called Jewish people "Nazis" and "parasites" who had funded the "Holohoax."[488] BBC also regularly receives criticism for refusing to call Hamas members terrorists despite their official UK designation as a terrorist organization.[489] Over a four month period during the Israel-Hamas war, Hamas was described as a "proscribed," "designated", or "recognized" terrorist organization just 409 times out of 12,459 times (3.2 percent.)[490] Like so many other outlets, the BBC repeatedly cites Hamas' "Gaza Ministry of Health" casualty numbers and reports of what's happening inside Gaza, with little to no representation of the facts reported by Israel.

RT

Russia Today (RT) is a Russian state-sponsored news outlet and covers conflicts and current events internationally. In every political conflict, it pushes Russia's own ideas of foreign policy. Particularly biased when it comes to Israel, RT often portrays the Jewish state as the source of all Palestinian suffering with no objective analysis of the region or regard to the role of Palestinian leadership. For example, in August 2024, RT ran the headline, "Dozens killed in Israeli airstrike on school," without mentioning that the majority of people killed in the strike were Hamas militants who had been hiding in the school which wasn't in session and was determined by the IDF to not contain civilians.[491] RT makes its anti-American position very clear, incorrectly labeling Israel's activities as somehow being involved with an American conspiracy to oppress other nations in the Middle East. This falls in line with the predominant narratives being peddled by the Russian regime, including support of the Islamic Republic of Iran, China, and apparently, Palestinian terrorists. RT has been banned in numerous locations, including permanently from YouTube, for its Russian state-affiliation.[492]

Press TV

Press TV is the primary media network of the Islamic Republic of Iran. Independent media is not allowed under the Islamic Republic's regime, only Press TV, which promotes blatantly antisemitic libels and cheerleads Islamic terrorism. Anything going around social media from Press TV should be considered wildly unreliable.[493] This, however, has not stopped radical Western public figures, including British Member of Parliament George Galloway as well as the former leader of the British Labour Party Jeremy Corbyn, from appearing on their talk shows.[494]

PRINT/LEGACY MEDIA

Because print media is the oldest form of journalism, and the medium itself connotes a certain definitive quality - a truth one can hold with their hands - it often carries a gravitas that other media lacks. Rightly or not, print media was once considered a bastion for "true journalism" where journalists abided by standards of practice: presenting both sides with impartiality and providing important context to understand the larger picture of current events. However, because of the newfound need for clicks, many say that the reporting gets less reliable, and when it comes to Israel, more harmful. Print media also often relies on and/or reprints from other sources, including the once respected **Associated Press**, (which called the noted terrorist leader of Hezobollah, Hassan Nasrallah, "a shrewd and charismatic leader" in his obituary.[495] The following are examples of how some of the larger print publications have exhibited bias.

The New York Times
The New York Times (NYT), though styled "the paper of record," has come under harsh scrutiny for their biased coverage during the conflict with Hamas, including their publishing of opinion pieces from the Hamas-appointed mayor of Gaza City while the terror group was still holding hostages.[496] NYT also regularly parrots information provided by Hamas in terms of casualty count without verifying or cross-checking that information, and in 2023, repeated Hamas' completely false claim that

Israel had bombed a hospital killing 500 people[497] (they were far from the only ones, as you'll see below). During the 2023 war, HonestReporting, a pro-Israel media watchdog, accused a freelance photographer of NYT of working with Hamas during the October 7th Massacre, and of knowing the details of the massacre some days before it happened, a claim NYT has denied.[498] After the assassination of Hezbollah chief Hassan Nasrallah, the New York Times said Nasrallah "maintained that there should be one Palestine with equality for Muslims, Jews, and Christians."[499]

The Washington Post

The Washington Post (WaPo) was once known for its critical coverage of important events. They released the famous Pentagon Papers which revealed unethical conduct by the U.S. Army in the Vietnam War, and uncovered evidence used to indict President Richard Nixon in the infamous Watergate scandal. However, in the last several years, the paper promotes a bias, especially when it comes to foreign policy and Israel. In the midst of the Israel-Hamas war, WaPo has come under fire for publishing an error-ridden front page story about premature Palestinian infants, which the editorial team had to heavily revise in an official editor's note.[500] At least two articles from top reporter Louisa Loveluck were followed up with heavy corrections,[501] and when the paper described Palestinians who had been arrested in Israel for killing innocent civilians as "captives," many made the argument that the paper had trespassed from journalism to political activism.[502] After the assassination of Hezbollah Chief Hassan Nasrallah, the Washington Post wrote: "Among his followers, Mr. Nasrallah was seen as a father figure, a moral compass and a political guide."[503] The paper referred to Hamas leader Ismail Haniyeh after his assassination in Tehran as "politically pragmatic."[504]

AL AHLI HOSPITAL BOMBING: A CASE STUDY

Ten days after the Massacre on October 17, 2023, the **Al Ahli Hospital** in Gaza exploded, and the world immediately blamed Israel for authorizing an airstrike. Within minutes, international media outlets published a report claiming that 500 Palestinians were killed, including AP, Reuters, BBC, CNN, Washington Post, New York Times, and many more. Al Jazeera Arabic was broadcasting from the scene within 15 minutes of the attack. The IDF announced instantly that they were investigating the incident, and within hours confirmed that the airstrike was not from their planes, nor was there any IDF activity in the vicinity at the time. It turned out that the terrorist organization Palestinian Islamic Jihad had launched a rocket at Israel from Gaza which fell short and detonated in the hospital parking lot. Between 40-50 people were reported killed, but not before the entire world accused Israel of killing hundreds of Palestinians.[505] To this day, public figures like Congresswoman Rashida Tlaib have posts on social media condemning Israel for the attack, which they didn't commit.[506]

Wall Street Journal
The Wall Street Journal is one of the only publications which has had relatively fair coverage that concentrates on the facts and presents multiple sides of the conflict. While one may not agree with every piece and certainly not every opinion piece, they are the best of all the international media options when it comes to impartiality on conflict in the Middle East.

THE INTERNET

Google and Artificial Intelligence
Google is the most popular search engine in the world, one which a federal judge has just declared to be an illegal monopoly.[507] The power it wields is so enormous that even the tiniest bias can affect whole industries and even elections. During their entry into the artificial intelligence space, Google unveiled an image generator called Gemini that was unable to generate historically accurate images. They had to shut down and restart.[508] When Open.ai, a different company, launched **ChatGPT**, if you asked it to tell a joke about Jews it would gladly do so, but if you asked it to tell a joke about Muslims it said it could not because that would be considered racist.[509] It is important to have a critical eye towards the ideological leanings of the organization from which you seek information.

Wikipedia

The original mission of Wikipedia was a great one: to encourage people to freely give their knowledge for the benefit of humankind. What could have been the world's greatest encyclopedia, however, has instead become a playground for activists to rewrite history to delegitimize the Jewish people and the Jews' claim to the land of Israel. It cannot be stressed enough – Jews are 0.2% of the world's population, and will never outnumber the army of indoctrinated college students and activist editors who will take down any information that they don't want to be true. Before the Israel-Hamas war of 2023, Wikipedia defined Zionism correctly, as a nationalist movement that sought to secure Jewish self-determination and liberation in their ancient homeland. But in 2024, the definition was changed to denote Zionism as a colonialist, "ethno-cultural" movement that called for the displacement of every Palestinian from the Land of Israel in order to form an exclusionary Jewish state.[510] This is a prime example of why outlets that can be edited by everyone and anyone cannot be trusted.

Wikipedia's misinformation campaign continues in the translated versions of pages in other languages. For example, when translated into English, the Arabic page on Adolph Hitler states that Hitler was merely the leader of Nazi Germany, listed as one of the 100 most influential figures of the 20th century, and skips over the bit about the extermination of 6 million Jews.[511] In 2024, after the assassination of Hamas political leader Ismael Haniyeh in Iran, Wikipedia described Haniyeh as a more "moderate, pragmatic" leader of Hamas, outraging Israelis, Jews, and their allies around the world[512] (Haniyeh is shown celebrating and praying during the October 7th Massacre in a widely circulated video).[513]

RADIO

During the ongoing Israel-Hamas war, editor at **NPR** (National Public Radio) Uri Berliner blew the whistle on the apparent bias against Israel and Jews among NPR's editorial team. Berliner noted how executives "highlighted the suffering of Palestinians at almost every turn while downplaying the atrocities, overlooking how Hamas intentionally puts Palestinian civilians in peril, and giving little weight to the explosion of antisemitic hate around the world."[514] Democracy Now is another radio station that has been subject to a great deal of criticism for its apparent anti-Jewish bias. Co-founder of Democracy Now, Amy Goodman, has interviewed anti-Israel extremists who advocate for the "fall of the Zionist project," who call the existence of Israel a "racist, criminal project," and who accuse Israel of practicing the crimes of apartheid and genocide.[515]

PODCASTS

In a sea of relative darkness, where algorithms skew public perception, one source of light is the world of deep discussion hosted on podcasts, which is essentially radio on demand. As of this writing, the search filter in the Apple Store uses no algorithms to skew what podcasts you will see, meaning you can listen to a variety of discussions about topics in depth to better flesh out your understanding on a number of issues. Excellent sources of information on the subject of Israel and the Jewish people from a variety of political standpoints include *Call Me Back with Dan Senor, Unpacking Israeli History, Israel Story, The Israel Policy Pod, Honestly with Bari Weiss, The Times of Israel: Daily Briefing, and We Should All Be Zionists.*

SPEAKING UP

While algorithms reward extremist content, the upside is that *every small interaction actually makes a difference*. It may feel hopeless, but if the Jewish community and its allies don't show up to the fight, the starting point of the debate shifts further away from the reality that Jews face when it comes to both Israel and antisemitism. Extremists embolden extremists. Engaging with social media when encountering lies about Israel benefits the Jewish people. It is also important to be judicious, as words written online can be permanent, even if you delete them. Don't get involved in discussions that jeopardize your safety or mental health. Here are some practical tips:

1. Don't list or give your physical address to anyone you interact with online.

2. Use "2-Step Verification" for all social media platforms to avoid your account being hacked.

3. Do not say anything that can be construed as hateful or racist.

4. Do not engage in personal attacks against individuals using strong and offensive language.

5. Take a second to think before anything is posted.
Ask yourself: *Do I have all the facts? Is my comment furthering a problematic narrative or contributing to a hostile online environment?*

6. Check the source of any claim or story being circulated.
If it's made up by an unknown individual, better to not engage, and if it's coming from a news platform, best to interrogate biases and to ascertain where the information was gathered from.

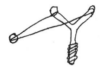

STAY STRONG

The twenty-four hour news cycle, where information is broadcasted all day, every day, by an infinite number of outlets to accommodate the millions of people in possession of computers and smartphones, has rendered us infinitely more informed, but simultaneously more radical and uncompromising in our worldviews. Algorithms and engagement farming by way of bots contributes to this reality, along with state-sanctioned (dis) information. All media has the power to influence geo-political events, which is why anyone looking to become involved in discussions and debates must be as informed and literate as possible.

9

THE CAMPUS

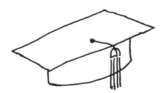

You are not alone.

In the 1880s, when Theodor Herzl was at the University of Vienna studying law, fellow members of his German national fraternity called a meeting to mourn the composer Richard Wagner, one of their heroes and a passionate Jew-hater. Herzl was shocked when his fraternity brothers erupted into antisemitic chants after their eulogies. At this time in history, the hatred of Jews inspired by Christianity was already considered old-fashioned and regressive, whereas antisemitism, which claimed the Jews were an inferior race, was thought to be based in science and therefore progressive. With the rise of discrimination against Jews that claimed to be of and for the modern era, Herzl began to struggle with what it meant to be a Jew in a quickly changing world. He resigned from his fraternity after months of inner turmoil: the fraternity had served as a major piece of his identity, his place of belonging.[516]

Later, after witnessing the Dreyfus Affair, Herzl wrote his seminal pamphlet, *The Jewish State*, and concluded that Europe's promise of emancipation, of granting its Jews civil rights and full equality with their neighbors, had failed. If even university students – the most educated members of German, Austrian, and French society – had succumbed to the poison of antisemitism, what hope was there for the rest of the population? Herzl understood that once these students, marinating in an ideology which blamed Jews for the world's ills, entered the higher ranks of society, it would create a very dangerous situation.

> *Am I stating what is not yet the case? Am I before my time? Are the sufferings of the Jews not yet grave enough? We shall see.*
> -Theodor Herzl Preface, *The Jewish State*, 1896

Herzl foresaw the unspeakable genocide to come. Indeed, during World War II, many European academics justified the Nazi regime using intellectual language that appealed to the educated classes, including the designation of "Aryan" as a superior German race.[517] Nobody should be shocked that Herzl's classmates established institutes and think tanks to study the racial inferiority of the Jews and other peoples.

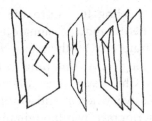

Today's Jewish people are not alone. This fever of antisemitism rises and falls within every generation. Just because it seems new or on the rise doesn't mean it has never happened before or that there is nothing to do about it. Start with knowing history.

COLLEGE ANTISEMITISM IN AMERICA, c. 1900s

After waves of Jewish immigration to America in the early 20th century, top universities including Columbia, Harvard, Stanford, Yale, and Princeton, famously employed **quotas**, or caps on the number of Jews that could enroll in classes each year, with some only lifted as recently as the 1960s with the passage of the Civil Rights Act. It was only in the middle of the 20th century that a true merit-based system rewarded young Jewish people with access to the golden ladder of American education.[518] The latter half of this century saw a flourishing in Jewish attendance at all respected universities. But since then, in the early 21st century, in the dawn of the age of social media, a new antisemitic ideology has infected American universities which views Jews not as a minority group but as an oppressive, white class. How ironic that not even a century earlier, Jews were excluded and even murdered for not being white. Now, reports of bias from Jewish students are at best dismissed and ignored and at worst delegitimize as hateful toward progressive students and/or students of color.

POST-OCTOBER 7TH MASSACRE CAMPUS PROTESTS

Since October 7th, American colleges have engaged in a spasm of antisemitism that has shocked the nation and the world. Radicalized pro-Hamas students at the likes of Columbia, George Washington, UCLA, and the University of Chicago have created no-go zones for Zionist students (a.k.a., Jews). They have called for the boycott of Jewish organizations, like **Hillel,** and Chabad, on campus.[519] They have harassed Jews attending Shabbat dinners and Jewish events on and off campus,[520] and have published flyers mandating the exclusion of "Zionists" from campus activities.[521] Organized protests include the shouting of *"Intifada, Revolution!," "From the River to the Sea,"* and the hanging of signs that say, "Israelis, go back home!"

In 2024, and in the name of justice and human rights, Jews once again represent the ills of society, just like they did in Theodor Herzl's age. The problem of antisemitism on college campuses isn't new, but when Israel engaged in a military operation to defend its very existence after the October 7th Massacre, the hatred boiled over. The rhetoric building in the classroom for the last decade made it inevitable.[522]

Hillel International, the largest Jewish organization operating at American universities today, marked a 700% increase in antisemitic incidents on campus.[524] From October 8, 2023 to June 30, 2024, 1,826 antisemitic incidents were recorded on campuses. After October 7th, before Israel had made any moves to defend itself or declared war against Hamas, Jewish college students were immediately confronted with an onslaught of antisemitism: at MIT, they were called Nazis and thrown out of study groups.[525] At Cornell, one student posted on social media: "if I see another synagogue rally for the zionist [sic] globalist genocidal apartheid dictatorial entity known as 'israel', [sic] i will bring an assault rifle to campus and shoot all you pig Jews," forcing the university to cancel classes.[526]

LANGUAGE IS IMPORTANT: "PRO-PALESTINIAN"

The news constantly refers to the protesters on university campuses as "pro-Palestinian," but framing it in this manner suggests that the other side is "anti-Palestinian" which is false. Furthermore, many of these protestors are singing and chanting the songs of martyrdom and praising terrorist organizations like Hamas and Hezbollah which is anti-Israel, not pro-Palestinian.[523] A genuine pro-Palestinian protest would be calling for Palestinians to be freed from Hamas, not supporting the organization that keeps their lives in permanent danger. Defending a terrorist organization that has launched and lost multiple wars and uses schools and hospitals as military bases, endangering civilians on a daily basis, does nothing to help the Palestinian people.

SPRING 2024 ENCAMPMENTS

Beginning in April 2024 large groups of students (along with outside agitators) gathered on the quads of American universities and set up tents, refusing to leave. The purported aim of these protests, expanded to over fifty-three campuses, was to force universities like Columbia and UCLA to divest from Israel (BDS), and suspend all economic investments between the university and Israeli companies and even more broadly, to boycott academic collaboration between researchers and professors on campus and academics at Israeli universities.[527] But the encampments, from their first day, were apparent to most observers as demonstrations of antisemitic hatred rather than objections to the university's connections with Israel.

Spring 2024 Encampments *(cont.)*

From the October 7th massacre to the present, the Anti-Defamation League reports 28 physical assaults, 201 instances of vandalism (including the tearing down of hostage posters,) 360 instances of harassment, and 73 instances that directly targeted Jewish student organizations including Hillel and Chabad.[554] Those looking for a database of each antisemitic incident on campus spanning the last several years can look to the *Amcha Initiative.*

APRIL 2024

- Stanford - students seen in Hamas memorabilia.[528]

- NYU Students chant: *"We Don't Want No Zionists Here!"*[529]

- Northwestern students hang a poster of a Jewish star (not an Israeli flag) with a large "X" over it.[530]

- According to a student lawsuit, a Jewish student wearing a Star of David necklace is harassed by a student yelling "Attention everyone! We have a Zionist who has entered the camp!" Another student wearing a yarmulke is spit on. Other students yell: "Zionists aren't welcome here, Zionists go home."[531]

- George Washington - student encampment hangs a sign reading: "Students will go back home when Israelis go back to Europe, their real homes."[532]

- A George Washington University student is photographed with a Palestinian flag and a sign reading "FINAL SOLUTION," referring to Hitler's extermination of the Jews.[533]

- Columbia University protest leader says, "Zionists don't deserve to live... be glad, be grateful, that I'm not out there murdering Zionists." This student was let off at the initial disciplinary hearing, only to be suspended when the Internet found out.[534]

- Flyers distributed at the University of Michigan read, "The third intifada is here," and, "Death to America."[535]

- Columbia students form a human chain to prevent "Zionists" from entering the encampment.[536]

- Columbia students yell, "*Yahood! Yahood!* ("Jews" in Arabic) Go back to Poland!"[537]

- Columbia student yells, "Remember October 7th! It will happen 5, 10, 15 more times!"[538]

- Columbia student yells, "We are Hamas" and others chanted: "Al-Qassam (in reference to Hamas's military wing) you make us proud, kill another soldier now!"[539]

- At Columbia, a Jewish student, while wearing his kippah, was followed to his dormitory by a group of students chanting, "Oh,You Zionist pig," and repeatedly called him a "baby killer" and made oinking noises at him.[540]

- Columbia, Jewish student wearing a kippah is followed on campus by a woman yelling "We have a Zionist here."[541]
- University of Texas Austin, a sign is posted reading "Zionists can choke and die on their own spit."[542]

- CUNY City College, protestors yelled at students: "We can smell the Zionist on you," "Israel go to hell," and "Two, four, six, eight, we don't want no Jewish state."[543]

- Colorado State, flyers advertising a Passover Seder at Chabad are vandalized with the word "*Satanic death cult.*"[544]

APRIL 2024 (CONT.)

- Princeton University, a student is seen brandishing a Hezbollah flag at a protest.[545]

- Ohio State University, students march through campus chanting: "Hey ho, hey ho, Zionists have got to go."[546]

- Harvard University students gather with faculty to shout, "Intifada, come to America!"[547]

MAY 2024

- George Washington University students at commencement ceremony yell in Arabic, "From the water to the water, Palestine is Arab."[548]

- "Free Palestine" spray-painted on the roof of a Jewish fraternity at Temple University.[549]

- A Jewish student is surrounded by five anti-Israel student protestors and beaten, taken to the ER.[550]

- University of North Carolina Chapel Hill, a Jewish student's mezuzah was torn down and the antisemitic slur "K*ke" was spray painted on his front door.[551]

- Reed College, a Jewish student's mezuzah is torn from their door, and the next day, a rock is thrown through his window.[552]

- DePaul University, students yell "Let's Go Hamas" in Arabic at a Jewish Mother's Day event.[553]

HOW RADICAL IDEAS PROPAGATE

How did these encampments arise? For years, universities overlooked the evident bias against Jewish students in classrooms and within their faculty, giving a pass to radical agitators, while punishing those who express bigotry against all other groups. Universities [particularly their Diversity, Equity, and Inclusion (DEI) departments] continue to address the complaints of Jewish students as simply criticism of Israel, and often frame Jewish students as radical rabble-rousers trying to silence those who disagree with them.[555] Radical ideas are often encouraged by the professors themselves, particularly in social science and political and Middle Eastern studies departments.[556] The publishing of unchecked false information on social media also plays a huge role. When those publishing are US Politicians, it makes matters worse, especially when people like US Representatives Ilham Omar, Rashida Tlaib, Jamal Bowman, and Alexandria Ocasio-Cortez all visited university encampments to show their support for the anti-Israel cause.[557]

Jewish Voice for Peace on Campus

Jewish Voice for Peace (JVP, which we touched upon in Chapter 7: *Lies and Misconceptions*) claims to represent Jewish voices on college campuses, but more often is led by non-Jewish students who wish to deceive unassuming students with a facade of Jewish allyship . JVP openly supports any effort against Israel including BDS and violent campaigns including Palestinian and Islamic terrorism (In September of 2024, JVP's University of Michigan chapter posted "Death to Israel is not just a threat. It is a moral imperative and the only acceptable solution. May the entire colony burn to the ground for good.")[558] JVP has also called to "Globalize the intifada" in official campaigns, published cartoons of Israelis drinking blood on their social media pages, praised Palestinians who have murdered Israelis and hijacked planes, and supported antisemitic projects to track where "Zionists" live and work in major U.S. cities.[559] Even if there are actual Jewish students present in a JVP chapter (or a Students for Justice in Palestine chapter), these students do not represent the majority Jewish opinion on campus. On the contrary, they are either plants or represent Jews buckling under the pressure of antisemites, turning into antisemites *themselves* for a false sense of security (see Chapter 7: *The Soviets*).

BARI WEISS

Bari Weiss, a critical voice on antisemitism today, was an undergraduate student at Columbia University in the early 2000s, where she experienced blatant, incendiary anti-Israel bias from her professors. With several other students, Weiss founded CAF, Columbians for Academic Freedom, which stressed that the behavior of faculty members, such as repeatedly shutting down the speech and opinions of students who disagreed with them on Israel, was a violation of academic standards.[560] Later on, Weiss wrote as an Opinion columnist for the *New York Times*, but in 2020, resigned from the Times Editorial Board on account of its bias against more centrist political opinions. Today, Weiss is the founder and Editor-in-Chief of the *Free Press*, an immensely popular publication of stories and opinions from all ideological viewpoints. Weiss is also the author of *How to Fight Antisemitism*, a frequent speaker for Jewish organizations and institutions, and a continual advocate for Jewish college students who feel sidelined by university culture.

INDISCRIMINATE OUTSIDE FUNDING

How did campus antisemitism become such a problem? One clue is the creation of **Title VI of the National Defense Education Act**, passed by Congress in 1956, which greenlit the establishment of research centers at American universities to facilitate study in foreign languages and cultures.[561] The government hoped to train American students to be experts in international relations in a rapidly modernizing world.

However, the Act also allowed foreign countries to invest heavily in foreign exchange programs: giving donations to American university departments to the tune of billions of dollars – and spreading specific ideas through teachers, students, and educational programming.

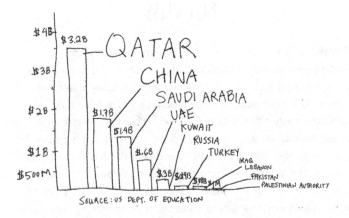

SOURCE: US DEPT. OF EDUCATION

We can directly trace the proliferation of antisemitic ideas on campus to donations from nations who are hostile to Israel. For example, the Qatari regime, a mass-exporter of antisemitism and host to terrorists, is the largest foreign donor to US universities, contributing $5.1 billion since 1986, with most donations being made in the past decade alone. The Institute for the Study of Global Antisemitism and Policy reported in November of 2023 that "there is a direct correlation between antisemitism and censored speech on campus and undocumented contributions from foreign governments, notably Qatar."[562]

"IT DEPENDS ON THE CONTEXT"

On December 5, 2023, the **United States House of Representatives Committee on Education** and the Workforce held a hearing with the presidents of Harvard University, the University of Pennsylvania (UPenn), and the Massachusetts Institute of Technology. The testimony from these officials created a firestorm in the media and online, as when Congresswoman Elise Stefanik asked whether calling for the genocide of the Jewish people was considered "harassment or intimidation," on campus, Liz Magill of UPenn stated that it depended on whether "statements turned into conduct." Claudine Gay of Harvard said that whether calls to kill the Jewish people en masse violated standards of conduct "depended on the context." Shortly thereafter, in response to a wave of criticism, both Magill and Gay resigned from their positions, but Gay kept her tenured professorship.[563]

In August 2024, a federal judge, Richard Stearns, said that Harvard had "failed its Jewish students," and ruled that a lawsuit filed against the university by its Jewish students, alleging the university had not acted with intent to stop the targeted harassment of Jewish students on campus, would move forward.[564]

LAWSUITS AGAINST UNIVERSITIES

In addition to the lawsuit filed against Harvard by Jewish students, similar lawsuits have been filed against New York University, Northwestern, Rutgers, Penn, UC Berkeley, Carnegie Mellon, Columbia University, MIT, and UCLA for their failure to combat Jew-hatred. A task force against antisemitism at UCLA recently found that Jewish students were repeatedly "harassed, threatened, and assaulted," including with images of swastikas around campus.[565] The task force at Columbia reports "crushing" discrimination against Jews and Israelis on campus, with instances of Jews being "driven out of their dorm rooms, chased off campus, compelled to hide their Jewish identity, ostracized by their peers and denigrated by faculty."[566]

ORIGINS OF STUDENTS FOR JUSTICE IN PALESTINE ON CAMPUS

Students for Justice in Palestine, an organization that spreads antisemitic campus hate speech under the guise of advocacy for the Palestinian people, has ties to dangerous actors overseas. *The Hill* reports: "[There is a] direct correlation between donations to universities by Qatar and other Gulf States and the presence of SJP groups on campus."[567] The founder of SJP, Hatem Bazian, also founded **American Muslims for Palestine (AMP)**,[568] and SJP continues to receive training and funding from AMP. [569]AMP's leadership is intimately linked with the Islamic Association for Palestine (IAP)[570] and its financial wing, the **Holy Land Foundation**, which was closed for its links to terrorist organizations (see: *U.S. vs. the Holy Land Foundation*).[571] The IAP has been found civilly liable for Hamas terror attacks,[572] while the HLF has sent millions of dollars directly to Hamas.[573]

U.S. VS. THE HOLY LAND FOUNDATION

The Holy Land Foundation for Relief and Development was a Texas-based non-profit charity with the stated mission of providing humanitarian aid to Palestinians. The newly created Department of Homeland Security, designed to crack down on terrorist-connected organizations in the U.S. after the 9/11 attacks, closed the HLF after substantial evidence came to light that the organization had provided resources and finances to terrorist organizations like Hamas and the PFLP.[574] In 2008-2009, the leaders of the HLF were prosecuted and convicted, receiving prison sentences from 15 to 65 years.[575]

ENGAGING CAMPUS ACTIVITIES

Despite the challenges facing Jews on campus, there are still numerous opportunities for students to foster a meaningful and enriching college experience by connecting with other Jews.

Hillel
You can find a Hillel chapter on almost every college campus in the country. Beginning in 1923 with its first chapter at the University of Illinois Urbana-Champaign, Hillel offers American Jewish young people an outlet to form and express their Jewish identity while they are studying. The organization focuses on Jewish pluralism, community, philanthropy, and activism against antisemitism on campus.[576]

Chabad
Chabad is catered toward students who are looking for a more observant Jewish outlet on campus. As discussed earlier in this book, Chabad is a sect of Hasidic Judaism which really took off in the United States during the leadership of Rabbi Menachel Menden Schneerson, who advocated reaching Jews where they are in regard to spiritual connection. Chabad on campus will regularly host Shabbat dinners, holiday celebrations, and Torah study.

AEPi

AEPi, or **Alpha Epsilon Pi**, is a Jewish fraternity that operates on more than 100 college campuses in the U.S.. Founded in 1913 at New York University by a group of twelve Jewish undergrads, AEPi today holds the mission of "developing the future leaders of the Jewish communities" which is demonstrated "every day through acts of brotherhood, Tzedakah, social awareness and support for Jewish communities and Israel."[577]

AEPhi

AePhi, or **Alpha Epsilon Phi**, is a Jewish sorority that works to provide Jewish female students with a strong sense of family on and off campus. AePhi is known for its civic action and philanthropic work, its advocacy for Israel, and its active alumni network. [578]

Birthright

Many have heard of this trip before — an all expenses paid, 10 day trip to Israel provided to every Jew in America between the ages of 18 and 26. **Birthright**, which runs multiple trips a year, caters to different college campuses, age groups, and identity groups (such as Reform and/or LGBT Jews, etc.) and is an excellent method of discovering Israel for oneself and becoming more connected to one's Jewish identity. Birthright also offers different styles of trips, from more outdoors-oriented to more religious.[579]

Young Judaea

Young Judea, America's oldest Zionist youth movement, offers a pluralistic, non-partisan, peer-led space for young American Jews to strengthen their Jewish identity by emphasizing the centrality of Israel in their lives. The organization offers leadership training, summer camp programming, and trips to Israel including gap years for soon-to-be college students.[580]

IS ATTENDING AN INSTITUTION WITH
ANTISEMITISM WORTH IT?

In the Jewish community there exists an ongoing debate about whether it is worth it to send young Jewish students into hostile learning environments. Some say: Why bother? Who needs the strife? College should be about learning and question why even put young Jews through this environment. Bari Weiss and others have even gone as far as creating the University of Austin to fashion an entirely new learning environment devoid of harmful discriminatory practices and wayward teachings.

The counter argument posits that Jewish students should not shy away from college life but, instead, embrace it with resilience and courage. Attending college provides Jewish students with the opportunity to be present, visible, and ready to advocate for themselves and their community. By participating in campus life, they can push back against hatred, educate others, and ensure that Jewish voices remain part of the broader academic and social discourse. In this sense, their presence is essential not only for their own education but for challenging antisemitism and fostering a more inclusive environment.

10

THE FUTURE

Regardless of how impossible circumstances may seem, the values and culture of the Jewish people endure. As dark as it may feel at times, whether on campus or in the streets of an American city, Jews today are the luckiest in history. Jews today have not only survived thousands of years as guests in other people's land, often with minimal or curtailed rights, but now they have their own country and army and have reconnected with brothers and sisters once scattered around the world. Even the smallest acts, like lighting candles on Friday nights or attending Bar/Bat Mitzvah ceremonies, demonstrate the strength of Jewish endurance. The Jewish people continue to pass down their unique way of living and important convictions to the later generations. Committing to Judaism enriches, sustains, and gives hope. As the biblical proverb says, "[Judaism] is the tree of life, to all who hold fast to it...."

How the Jewish people fare depends on where they are in the world, and in which direction the political winds are blowing. The Jewish people are *always* better off in countries that adhere to the principles of tolerance and equal rights for all. Unfortunately, all over the world today, leaders on both the right and left challenge democratic order and attempt to rally supporters with conspiracy theories and "us vs. them" rhetoric, which has never ended well for the Jews.

In the **Book of Esther**, preceding a call to kill all the Jews, Haman says:

> *There is a certain people scattered and dispersed among the people in all the provinces of your kingdom; their laws are different from all other people's, and they do not keep the king's laws. Therefore it is not fitting for the king to let them remain.*[581]

In the Diaspora, whenever a society gets sick, the Jews are the first to blame. Therefore, the Jewish people should always stand up to autocratic rulers and corrupt forms of government wherever they appear and to strive for a world that is committed to human rights and freedom.

MARK TWAIN

The Egyptian, the Babylonian, and the Persian rose, filled the planet with sound and splendor, then faded to dream-stuff and passed away; the Greek and the Roman followed, and made a vast noise, and they are gone; other peoples have sprung up and held their torch high for a time, but it burned out, and they sit in twilight now, or have vanished. The Jew saw them all, beat them all, and is now what he always was, exhibiting no decadence, no infirmities of age, no weakening of his parts, no slowing of his energies, no dulling of his alert and aggressive mind. All things are mortal but the Jew; all other forces pass, but he remains. What is the secret of his immortality?

- Mark Twain, "Concerning The Jews," 1899

The Future of American Jews

There are approximately 7.5 million Jews in America, just over the number of those in Israel. Despite facing some tough conversations, there are thousands of American Jewish organizations and synagogues operating from coast to coast, specializing in religion, politics, and education, or simply connecting Jews to other Jews. American Jews are active in

The Future of American Jews *(cont.)*

every sphere of public life and are important contributors to national conversations and ideas for the future. If American Jews feel proud of this beating heart, and if they commit to fighting against those who call for not only the death of Israel (which directly impacts American Jews) but also for the death of America and its democratic institutions, there is every reason to feel excited about the future.

The Future of French Jews

France has the largest population of Jews after Israel and the United States, numbering at about 500,000. France was the first country to emancipate (grant political rights to) its Jews in the late 1700s, which is why there still exists a strong attachment between France and its Jews.[582] Unfortunately, in the last several decades, rising antisemitism on both the right and left (antisemitic acts in France nearly quadrupled in the year 2023 alone)[583] has led to the emigration of tens of thousands of French Jews, mainly to Israel. At the time of this writing, a play is showing on the Broadway stage called *Prayer for the French Republic*, written by Jewish playwright Josh Harmon, which explores the tension of French and Jewish identity in history and in the present day. The future of French Jewry is uncertain, yet a thriving community endures, just like the larger, global Jewish community.

The Future of British Jews

The Jews of Great Britain also have strong attachments to their country, as Britain was historically far more tolerant to its Jewish minority than other countries in Europe. Although there are only about 275,000 Jews in Britain, the community excels in the fields of politics, law, entertainment, and medicine.[584] Britain's Jewish community underwent a major ordeal in 2019 when Jeremy Corbyn ran as leader of the Labour Party, coming within a hairbreadth of becoming Prime Minister. Corbyn had been personally accused of antisemitism many times, and under his leadership, his party was found guilty by the European Commission of Human Rights of "institutional antisemitism," usually justified by supporters as "strong criticism of Israel."[585]

The Future of South African Jews

Jews have been trickling out of South Africa and into countries like Israel, Great Britain, and the United States for decades. Jews were instrumental in the fight to topple South African apartheid, but since the fall of the racist system, the "rainbow nation" has failed to extend tolerance to its Jews. The leading South African political party, the **African National Congress (ANC)**, is strongly influenced by Soviet ideas of anti-Zionism, and has proven sympathetic to the Iranian regime in recent years. Recently, the ANC's accusation of genocide against Israel at the International Criminal Court and a recent law that active members of the IDF will be arrested upon arrival in the country has strained the Jewish community's sense of security to a breaking point. Many wonder if South Africa will follow the fate of the Middle East soon, adopting anti-Zionism as state-policy, and therefore purging its Jewish population.[586]

The Future of Russian and Ukrainian Jews

Russia and Ukraine are currently at war, and Jews on both sides of the front find themselves in a political crossfire and, like so many Jews in our history, have chosen to leave. Though Ukraine and Russia boast more Jewish history than probably any other place on the planet, since World War II, prospects for a Jewish future in Eastern Europe have grown more and more dim, made more evident by the **Cold War** and now the war in Ukraine. The places that have seen a jump in Russian/Ukrainian Jewish immigration in the past several years are Israel and the United States.

THE FUTURE OF ISRAEL

This book is being written on the eve of Israel's 76th anniversary. On Independence Day, Yom Ha'atzmaut, Jews will dance in the streets to celebrate the triumph of the Jewish people in re-establishing themselves in their ancient homeland. Like all countries, but especially in Israel, people strive to resolve ethnic and religious tensions, land disputes, and historical grievances without violence. Israel has to protect the Jewish people on her land and make room for the growing movement of Jews coming from the Diaspora. It has to continue to make peace with its neighbors. Just like American Jews, Israelis will continue refining and defining its future as a safe haven for Jews in their ancestral homeland.

Abraham Accords

Amidst all the darkness, there are glimmers of hope for coexistence. In the United Arab Emirates, there is a synagogue, a mosque, and a church – structured in the shape of a triangle, symbolizing unity and peace with the three Abrahamic religions. In Dubai, there is even a new Holocaust Museum, designed to educate the people of the UAE on the horrors inflicted upon the Jewish people.[587] **Textbooks** in the UAE and Bahrain have been amended to remove antisemitic rhetoric and conspiracy theories originally adopted by the Arab world, and now include the history of the Jewish people and Israel. These changes would have been inconceivable a short time ago.[588]

The Abraham Accords, signed in 2020 between Israel, the UAE, and Bahrain, officially normalized relations between the three countries. The growing and continuing threat posed by the Islamic Republic of Iran has caused the Sunni states to align with the strategic interests of Israel. Secondly, there is increasing interest in the Middle East regarding how modernity can be fused into Islam in order to produce prosperous countries. With more tolerant thinking and openness to liberal reform comes more tolerance for and acceptance of the story of the Jewish people. Third, there is a growing understanding that Palestinian rejectionism has never produced anything good for the Palestinians, and that in the 21st century, opposition against the State of Israel existing in any borders is a main function of the Iranian regime's ideology which becomes more disconnected from the Arab world's priorities by the day.

The Future of Iran and Israeli Relations

When the Islamic Republic ceases to exist, a new Iran will rise from its defeat. Many Iranian people, both in Iran and the Diaspora, have expressed incredible allyship with the Jewish people and Israel for years, some simultaneously risking their lives by protesting the regime in the streets of Tehran.[589] The longstanding friendship between the Iranian and Jewish people dates back thousands of years to the time of Cyrus the Great, the Persian ruler who encouraged Jews to return to Jerusalem and rebuild the Second Temple. Only with the ascension of the Islamic Republic of Iran in 1979 did relations between the two groups seemingly fracture. Yet today, even though the two nations are believed to be enemies, the majority of the Iranian people have no issue with Israel and in fact support the Jewish state.[590]

The benefits for both countries would be tremendous. Israel's start-up nation technology could help Iran solve some of their greatest environmental crises. Israel would benefit from doing business with a market of 80 million people.

A Final Letter to the Reader

In this book, we have sought to fill the gaps of knowledge about subjects that the average Jewish college student might confront on campus. The first three chapters are a brief history and overview of what it means to be Jewish, about the nation of Israel and the Middle East. In chapters four, five, and six, we give a deep dive into the subjects that require substance and evidence, including the situation in the West Bank and Gaza and current obstacles for peace. We break down how UNRWA colludes with terrorist groups to fund warfare and indoctrination under the pretense of helping "refugees," who aren't really refugees. We then show the sad, once hopeful, trajectory, of the now decrepit United Nations which has devolved into a theater for dictatorial regimes to sanitize and distract from their own failing leadership. Chapters seven, eight, and nine provide an overview of common lies and how they are also promulgated by the media and on the campus, which has recently become a cauldron of extremist ideologies, aided heavily by foreign funding.

This last chapter, "The Future," has focused on the progress and the obstacles that lay before us. The October 7th massacre, as horrific as it was, also provided clarity about the perpetrators of good and evil in the world. So much has even happened since we started writing this book: Hezbollah and Hamas have been seriously degraded, Bashar al-Assad the butcher of Syria, has fallen, and the Islamic Republic of Iran has revealed itself to be a paper tiger with a rapidly approaching expiration date. It is hard for the Western mind to comprehend a religious fundamentalist worldview found in facets of Islam, where fulfillment comes when the Jews are either converted or dead. The West will always have a rude awakening when it misinterprets such dark and perverse desires as merely a hardened negotiating position which might change with exchange of land or money. Radicals might even create the illusion of softening only to enact the final desire or mission at a later date. And it is wise to remember that what starts with the persecution of Jews never ends with only Jews. Yet despite all the many trials and hardships Jews have endured for thousands of years, and in the recent past, our civilization has survived millennia and has never been stronger than it is today.

ACTIONS YOU CAN TAKE

When to Argue and How
It is crucial to know when, where, and how to deploy the knowledge gathered in this book. One has to assume that ultimately people mean well, but have drawn opinions from different sets of data, and some have suffered outright indoctrination from social media, news and academia. If one senses that there is an opening in another person's mind to new information then one should seize the opportunity to educate others. Some who attack the Jewish people and Israel do so out of malice or are so steeped in the countless lies and misconceptions that as frustrating as it may seem, it just might not be worth it.

Speak Out, but Be Wise
Our generation has the amazing ability to publish our thoughts for millions of people all over the world to see. Yet we now live in an era when many things that are said cannot be unsaid, as the Internet lasts forever. When engaging with controversial topics with classmates, whether in the lecture hall or online, think before a claim is made, and to only trust reliable sources when presenting an argument. Remember that many people in discussions about religion and politics are on a steady diet of misinformation from the media and/or academia. Some might not be acting in good faith. The goal should be to connect with people who are genuinely interested in learning more.

Connect to Jewish Community On Campus

Most college campuses at American universities have a Jewish community, and many have a robust and active presence. Check out *Campus Activities to Keep You Engaged* in the previous chapter for information about Jewish life on your campus. Connecting with Jewish life is a great avenue to feel supported and celebrated while studying, and it's also a proven method to make new friends. We're also betting that you'll learn a great deal more about your own Judaism from Jewish classmates and teachers.

Join a Birthright Trip

Birthright is one of the most rewarding and successful Jewish education programs in history. Since its founding in 1999, over 850,000 diaspora Jews have had the opportunity to go on an all-expenses paid trip to Israel with their college or the local Jewish community. You can learn more by going to birthright.org. Since October 7th, Birthright also created a thriving volunteer program for cohorts of people from the same geographical location to help with farming and helping displaced families in Israel.

Study in Israel

There are alternatives to making *aliyah* (moving to Israel) that can connect you to your Jewish *misphacha* (family) overseas. Studying in Israel, taking a gap year between high school and college, studying abroad, or pursuing a bachelor's/master's degree in the Jewish homeland is a wonderful (and comparatively cheap) experience that enriches the lives of many young Jews and non-Jews alike. There are so many benefits: improving your Hebrew, making new friends, studying in a new and diverse place, or simply getting out of your comfort zone. Also, it's important to repeat: the only way to understand Israel is to see Israel.

Learn Hebrew

There are so many wonders of the survival of the Jewish people but one cannot understate the miracle of the resurrection of the ancient language of Hebrew that allows it exist as a modern language today. Even the early Zionists thought the idea of Hebrew as the official language of the Jewish state as too far-fetched, but thanks to Eliezer Ben Yehuda, the same characters inscribed on the tablets from Mount Sinai are also the ones broadcasted from the loud speakers of the plane that descends into Israel on your first trip to Tel Aviv. Learning Hebrew will connect you with Israel as well as deepen your understanding of Judaism.

Family, Friends, Community

Connecting with one's family during the Jewish holidays, whether it be once a week during Shabbat or once a year during Yom Kippur, is a powerful way to feel more connected to your people. Likewise, spending more time with Jewish friends and in Jewish community spaces will expand your understanding of Judaism, Israeli culture, and the different ways to be Jewish in the 21st century. Jewish community centers and synagogues often host important events aimed at education, philanthropy, and religious enrichment for Jews of all backgrounds regardless of their level of religious observance.

Continue to Educate Yourself

Become a good advocate for Israel and the Jewish people by learning more. Find the author's favorite books and podcasts at **10ThingsEveryJewShouldKnow.com** that will ease the journey.

Be Bold: Make Aliyah

Move to Israel. We understand that this is a challenging task: it may not be possible at the moment due to a job, family, finances, and other commitments. But the benefit to a Jewish soul in moving to the Jewish homeland cannot be understated, for it aligns one spiritually to the Jewish faith, politically to the place where the Jewish people are deciding their own future, and physically to a diverse and ever-evolving Jewish community. Learning Hebrew, serving in the army, raising a family, and learning more about how different types of Jews and Israelis of all stripes live will be a formative life decision that connects one to the long history of the Jewish people.

BIBLIOGRAPHY

For the complete bibliography with 590 citations, go to
10ThingsEveryJewShouldKnow.com/**bibliography**

INDEX

ABOUT THE AUTHORS

EMILY SCHRADER

Emily Schrader, co-author, is an award-winning American-Israeli journalist and human rights activist focusing on Israeli and Iranian affairs. She is an anchor at *ILTV News* and a senior correspondent at *Ynet News*. Schrader sits on the executive board of the Institute for Voices of Liberty, a think tank focused on European and American policy with Iran, and advises lawmakers in North America and Europe, especially related to Tehran's terror proxies in the Middle East. She holds a B.A. in Political Science from University of Southern California and an M.A. in Political Communications from Tel Aviv University. She has over 400,000 followers on social media, and is the recipient of the 2023 Nefesh b'Nefesh Bonei Zion award for Young Leadership. In 2023, Schrader was named by the *Algemeiner* as one of the top 100 voices positively influencing Jewish life. Find her @EmilyInTelAviv.
emilyschrader.net

BLAKE FLAYTON

Blake Flayton, co-author, is a writer and activist living in Tel Aviv. While a student at George Washington University, Blake published an op-ed in *The New York Times* on campus antisemitism and started freelancing for several other publications, specifically writing about the phenomenon of left-wing anti-Zionism. After graduating, Blake served as a weekly columnist for the *Jewish Journal* of Los Angeles and made Aliyah to Israel in 2022. Today, Blake writes for the Substack blog *Bourgeois Nationalist* while pursuing a Master's Degree in Middle Eastern Religion and Politics at Bar-Ilan University. He also works with Dr. Einat Wilf, former member of Knesset, on producing Jewish educational content including the *We Should All Be Zionists* podcast. Find him @blakeflayton.
bflayton.substack.com

KIMBERLY BROOKS

Kimberly Brooks, editor/illustrator, is a contemporary American artist whose work has been showcased in museums and galleries internationally. Books about her work include *Brazen* and *Fever Dreams*. She is also the author and illustrator of *The New Oil Painting* (Chronicle Books). She has published over seventy essays on art and creativity. She is the regular host of *First Person Artist*, an interview series. To view her work and other projects, visit:
kimberlybrooks.com

STAY INVOLVED

RESOURCES

Recommended books, podcasts, and articles:
10ThingsEveryJewShouldKnow.com / **resources**

BIBLIOGRAPHY

10ThingsEveryJewShouldKnow.com / **bibliography**

ORDER BOOKS

10ThingsEveryJewShouldKnow.com / **bookorders**

PODCAST

10ThingsEveryJewShouldKnow.com / **podcast**

CONTACT

10ThingsEveryJewShouldKnow.com / **contact**

10ThingsEveryJewShouldKnow.com

Made in the USA
Monee, IL
09 May 2025

17072038R00177